HOMELAND SECURITY
OPERATIONAL ANALYSIS CENTER

Human Smuggling and Associated Revenues

What Do or Can We Know About Routes from Central America to the United States?

VICTORIA A. GREENFIELD, BLAS NUÑEZ-NETO, IAN MITCH, JOSEPH C. CHANG, ETIENNE ROSAS

Published in 2019

Preface

This report presents initial findings from a scoping study titled "Economic Value of Human Smuggling to Transnational Criminal Organizations." A primary goal of this study, which was completed in less than two months, was to develop a preliminary estimate of transnational criminal organizations' (TCOs') revenues from smuggling migrants from the Northern Triangle region of Central America—consisting of Guatemala, Honduras, and El Salvador—to the United States. In addition, we sought to establish what is known or knowable about the characteristics, including the structure, operations, and financing, of TCOs that engage in human smuggling along those routes.

From the start, we intended to frame any revenue estimate as a range to accommodate a short study period and considerable uncertainty; however, as the research progressed, we encountered further challenges. We learned that human smuggling involves many different types of actors and that we could not credibly distinguish most TCOs' activities and revenues from those of other actors, including ad hoc groups and independent operators, that engage in human smuggling. Thus, we could provide, at best, a range for revenues to all types of smugglers, largely irrespective of their affiliations.

Although our findings are subject to a high degree of uncertainty, they represent a contribution to the evidence base informing ongoing U.S. government efforts to address threats to homeland security posed by TCOs and other actors that participate in human smuggling. The U.S. Department of Homeland Security (DHS) can use the insights provided in this report regarding the characteristics of human-smuggling operations to help shape policies and prioritize resources to counter that threat. The findings will also be of interest to others in the policy community, including those who undertake research on its behalf.

This research was sponsored by DHS's Science and Technology Directorate and conducted within the Strategy, Policy, and Operations Program of the Homeland Security Operational Analysis Center federally funded research and development center (FFRDC).

About the Homeland Security Operational Analysis Center

The Homeland Security Act of 2002 (Section 305 of Public Law 107-296, as codified at 6 U.S.C. § 185), authorizes the Secretary of Homeland Security, acting through the Under Secretary for Science and Technology, to establish one or more FFRDCs to provide independent analysis of homeland security issues. The RAND Corporation operates the Homeland Security Operational Analysis Center (HSOAC) as an FFRDC for the U.S. Department of Homeland Security (DHS) under contract HSHQDC-16-D-00007.

The HSOAC FFRDC provides the government with independent and objective analyses and advice in core areas important to the department in support of policy development, decisionmaking, alternative approaches, and new ideas on issues of significance. The HSOAC FFRDC also works with and supports other federal, state, local, tribal, and public- and private-sector organizations that make up the homeland security enterprise. The HSOAC FFRDC's research is undertaken by mutual consent with DHS and is organized as a set of discrete tasks. This report presents the results of research and analysis conducted under 70RSAT18FR0000145, the Economic Value of Human Smuggling to Transnational Criminal Organizations.

The results presented in this report do not necessarily reflect official DHS opinion or policy.

For more information on HSOAC, see www.rand.org/hsoac.

For more information on this publication, visit www.rand.org/t/RR2852.

Contents

Figures

Tables

Summary

This report presents initial findings from a scoping study titled "Economic Value of Human Smuggling to Transnational Criminal Organizations." A primary goal of this study was to develop a preliminary estimate of transnational criminal organizations' (TCOs') revenues from smuggling unlawful migrants from the Northern Triangle (NT) region of Central America—consisting of Guatemala, Honduras, and El Salvador—to the United States. Given a tight deadline and the inherent challenges of research on illicit activities, we recognized the infeasibility of developing a point estimate for revenue and, instead, sought to develop a range of estimates. We also sought to establish what is known or knowable about the characteristics, including structure, operations, and financing, of TCOs that engage in human smuggling along routes from the NT to the United States and the markets in which they operate.

Providing the U.S. Department of Homeland Security (DHS) with a better understanding of how TCOs and other actors that participate in human smuggling are structured, do business, and are financed could help inform efforts to investigate and disrupt them and to make decisions about how to allocate resources to those efforts. For example, such understanding could help DHS identify TCOs' vulnerabilities and supply evidence to weigh the benefits of action. However, our interviews with subject-matter experts (SMEs), review of the literature, and data analysis indicated that many different types of smugglers are involved in human smuggling and that we could not credibly distinguish the activities and revenues of TCOs that smuggle humans ("human-smuggling TCOs") from those of independent operators, ad hoc groups, and others who also engage in human smuggling.

Thus, we could not consider the characteristics of human-smuggling TCOs in isolation, nor could we provide a preliminary estimate—or even a range of estimates—for smuggling revenues that flow solely to these TCOs. Instead, we developed a range for the "aggregate" revenues that flow to all types of smugglers, including not just TCOs but also independent operators, ad hoc groups, and other actors. Separately, we were able to identify and evaluate the "taxes," or *pisos*, that migrants pay to drug-trafficking TCOs for the right to pass through their territories en route to the United States and at the U.S.-Mexico border. Revenues from *pisos* appear to be modest compared with revenues from smuggling.

This summary presents an overview of our findings on the characteristics of human smugglers that operate along routes from the NT to the United States, as well as the characteristics of smuggling, more generally, and preliminary estimates of revenues from this activity along with drug-trafficking TCOs' *piso* collections.

The Characteristics of Human Smuggling

We found that many different types of smugglers—or "actors"—are involved in moving unlawful migrants from the NT to the United States and that they provide similarly wide-ranging services. These actors comprise a spectrum, spanning from independent operators who move unlawful migrants along particular segments of the route or offer other discrete services (e.g., a taxi driver based out of one town that ferries migrants to the next major town) to more formally structured networks that may include a central figure who coordinates smuggling efforts along the entire route.

There is some debate in the literature about the extent to which groups of smugglers are becoming more professional and sophisticated, particularly in light of possible increases in smuggling fees. However, our analysis suggests that many, if not most, of these groups are loosely organized, nonhierarchical, and generally do not maintain a definable command structure. The diversity and proliferation of individuals and groups involved in some aspect of human smuggling make it challenging to identify the extent to which these activities are conducted by actual TCOs.

Taxonomy of Human Smugglers

Table S.1 presents a taxonomy of types actors engaged in human smuggling, based on our review of the literature, including academic articles, press reports, and reports written by government agencies, nongovernmental organizations, and multilateral entities and interviews with SMEs. The table starts with the least organized types of smugglers and ends with the most organized types. At each level, actors differ by organizational cohesion, membership, and geographic dispersion along smuggling corridors.

Table S.1. The Spectrum of Actors Engaged in Human Smuggling

Type of Actor	Organizational Structure	Services	Group Membership	Geographic Reach
Independent operators	One "cell" composed of one or a few individuals	Provide a discrete service (e.g., transportation or lodging)	Do not generally work with other cells or actors	Generally work in one location, or between two locations
Ad hoc groups	Two or more independent operators that may not always work together	Provide multiple, complementary services	Generally unaware of other actors and groups more than one degree of separation removed	Work in one, two, or more locations
Loose networks	A larger number of small groups that usually work together	May provide end-to-end service along the full route or a portion of the route	Members may know only a limited number of other members	Working in many locations, potentially the full route
More-formal networks	A central figure who coordinates groups that consistently work together	Provide end-to-end services	Members generally know each other	Working along the full route

Many of the actors engaged in human smuggling do not appear to meet the statutory definition of a TCO. For example, few of the actors shown in Table S.1 appear to feature "self-perpetuating associations" that protect their activities through "a pattern of corruption and/or violence," with a "transnational organizational structure," as articulated in 10 U.S.C. § 284(i)(6). Adding another layer of complication, smugglers commonly move between levels or can operate at more than one level along the spectrum, depending on their opportunities. In fact, many of these actors can be thought of as subcontractors, that might offer their services to different networks, groups, or other independent operators at the same time. Partly for these reasons, we were largely unable to disentangle the activities and revenues of TCOs from those of other actors that engage in human smuggling.

Human-Smuggling Services and Roles

The broad spectrum of actors engaged in human smuggling supports a wide range of service options for unlawful migrants. At one end of the range, the migrants can opt for "all-inclusive" or "end-to-end" arrangements, in which migrants pay a large fee to a network that arranges all their travel—and may even send a representative to travel with them—that can amount to upward of $10,000. At the other end, migrants can "pay as they go" and travel on their own for portions of the route and then connect with local smugglers to pay for transportation and logistical support for other portions of the route, which can cost much less. There is no consensus in the literature or among SMEs concerning what percentage of migrants uses "all-inclusive" arrangements and what percentage chooses to "pay as they go."

Smugglers typically fill a number of roles, whether they are working as independent operators or as part of a group or network. Depending on the sophistication of the operation, individuals or small groups of people (sometimes referred to as a *cell* by law enforcement) can fill these roles. Below is a brief description of the key roles:

- **Facilitation/coordination.** Identify and recruit migrants, collect up-front fees, pay other smuggling organizations during the migrants' journey, and coordinate some or all the migrants' travel from their source country to their final destination.
- **Transportation.** Transport migrants from one location to another along the route north using conveyances that range from taxis to charter buses and tractor-trailers.
- **Logistics/stash houses.** Provide logistical support, often in the form of lodging or "stash houses" where migrants can take shelter for a few days or even a few weeks.
- **Fraudulent documents.** Provide unlawful migrants with fraudulent documents, including Mexican visas, national identity cards, or birth certificates, to facilitate their travel through Mexico, create synthetic families, or avoid detention.
- **Footguides/coyotes/*polleros*.** Guide migrants seeking to avoid detection while entering the United States—generally single adults—across the border between ports of entry in order to circumvent border security personnel.

Relationship Between Human Smuggling and Drug Trafficking

A handful of drug-trafficking organizations that are commonly identified as TCOs maintain control of the primary trafficking corridors into the United States, which allows them to regulate and tax illicit trade through their territory. Controlling prime smuggling territory also affords the drug traffickers an opportunity to charge migrants a "tax," or *piso*, for the right to pass through. According to U.S. government sources, it is all but impossible for migrants to cross some sections of the border, particularly those most tightly controlled by the drug traffickers, without paying the *piso*. Collecting the *piso* requires fairly extensive regulation of migrants passing through a drug-trafficking organization's territory, pointing to coordination between human smugglers and drug traffickers before a migrant reaches the U.S.-Mexico border. The *piso* is perhaps the clearest example of identifiable TCO earnings that can be associated with human smuggling, even if it is not "smuggling revenue," per se. In addition to coordinating *piso* collections, there are some reports that drug-trafficking TCOs coordinate unlawful migrants' border crossing to divert attention from other illicit activities, and that they may recruit or coerce some migrants into carrying drugs for them. Beyond these activities, however, there is little evidence that drug-trafficking TCOs are involved in human smuggling writ large.

Preliminary Findings on Revenue Estimation

Although we could neither develop a point estimate for revenues from smuggling unlawful migrants from the NT to the United States nor attribute such revenues to particular types of smugglers, we were able to use data from DHS and other sources to construct a range of preliminary estimates of revenue to all smugglers, without regard to their type. Separately, we were able to identify migrants' payments to drug-trafficking TCOs, specifically, for passing through these TCOs' territories.

Figure S.1 depicts the flows of revenues associated with human smuggling to human smugglers of all types, including TCOs, and to drug-trafficking TCOs. The larger oval to the right represents the former, designated as "aggregate" smuggling revenue, and the smaller oval to the left represents the latter, designated as "tax" revenue. The intersection of the two ovals represents instances in which smuggling fees cover the tax.

Figure S.1. Revenues to and Types of Actors Engaged in Human Smuggling

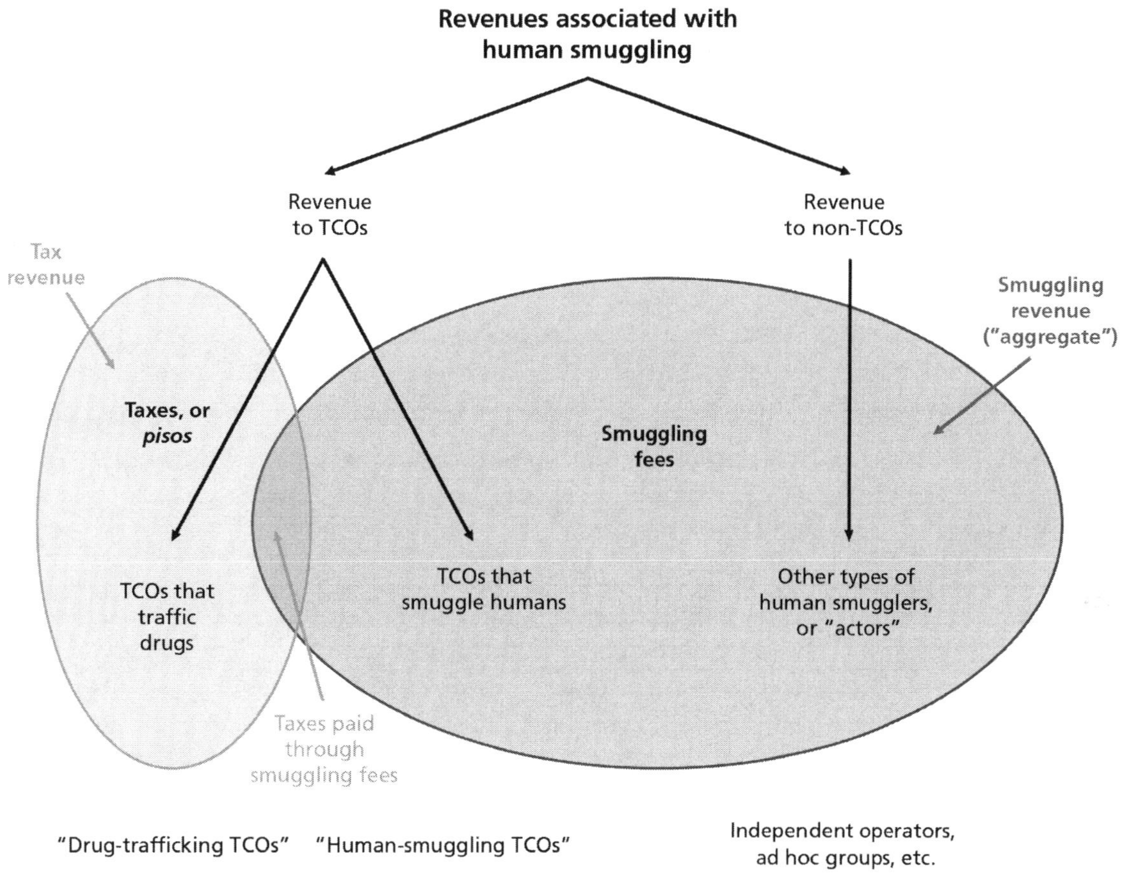

To estimate revenue to all types of human smugglers (i.e., aggregate smuggling revenue) along routes from the NT to the United States, we required data on three variables: (1) the number of unlawful migrants along a route, (2) the percentage of those migrants who hire smugglers, and (3) the typical payments made, per migrant, to smugglers. We defined three general routes, by country of origin, as "Guatemala–United States," "Honduras–United States," and "El Salvador–United States." We also produced an ancillary, preliminary estimate of drug-trafficking TCOs' *piso* collections.

We analyzed data from 2015–2017 and earlier, but we worked primarily with data from the most recent available year, i.e., 2017, for the smuggling revenue and tax estimates.

Flows of Unlawful Migrants

To estimate the flow of unlawful migrants from the NT to the United States, we used data on apprehensions and other activity at the U.S.-Mexico border, between ports of entry (POEs), that are collected by the U.S. Border Patrol and data from an analysis of apprehension rates, also between POEs, reported in a 2017 DHS Office of Immigration Statistics study. We tried four different estimation methods (see Appendix C), using different combinations of these data, to produce a range of estimates for unlawful migration from Guatemala, Honduras, and El Salvador. By that approach, we found that the flow of unlawful migrants from the NT to the United States in 2017 could have ranged from about 218,000 to about 345,000 between POEs.

Percentage of Unlawful Migrants Hiring Smugglers

To estimate the percentage of unlawful migrants who hire smugglers along the routes, we drew on data from DHS and from a survey of migrants called the Encuesta sobre Migración en la Frontera Sur de México, which translates to "Survey of Migration at Mexico's Southern Border" (we will refer to it by its Spanish abbreviation, EMIF Sur). This survey is conducted at the Mexico-Guatemala border by the Colegio de la Frontera Norte, which is located in Mexico. Because the DHS data on migrants' use of smugglers might fail to capture a substantial amount of smuggling activity (see Chapter 3), the DHS data suggest a lower bound. From the two sources, we concluded that about one-quarter to two-thirds of unlawful migrants from the NT might have hired smugglers in recent years, with some variation by country of origin.

Human-Smuggling Fees and Payments

For this calculation, we also drew from DHS and EMIF Sur data and turned to other sources, including our own interviews with SMEs. We used the DHS data to calculate mean and median smuggling fees, by country of origin, as reported to U.S. Border Patrol agents by unlawful migrants who are apprehended at the U.S.-Mexico border, between POEs. We also looked at the EMIF Sur data on unlawful migrants' actual and agreed payments to smugglers along routes from the NT to and into the United States. The results using the EMIF Sur data, which might include some unrealized payments and more transit in the United States, were substantially higher than the results using the DHS data and—importantly—better aligned with anecdotal evidence and most SME perspectives.

Taking the properties of the DHS and EMIF Sur data into account, we chose to work with the median values for the fees for transit from each country in 2017 to create ranges. Route by route, the median value from the DHS data represented the low end of the range, and the median value from the EMIF Sur data represented the high end (see Figure S.2).

Figure S.2. Median Values of Northern Triangle Migrants' Payments to Smugglers in 2017, by Country of Origin and Data Source (in U.S. dollars)

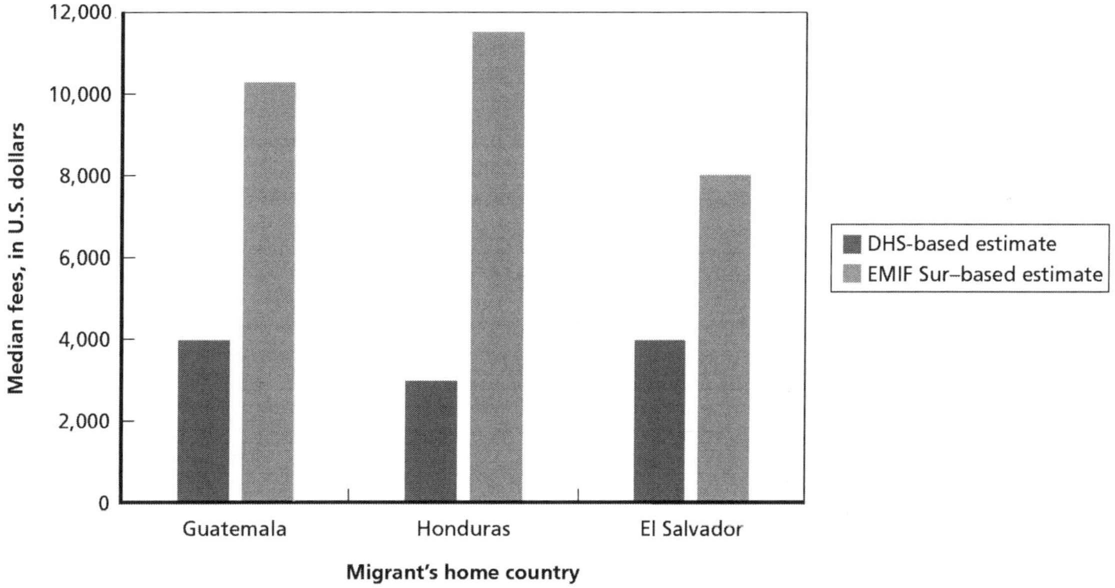

SOURCES: Author estimates based on EMIF Sur calendar-year data (EMIF, undated-a) and fiscal-year data provided by DHS.
NOTE: Cost estimates are in nominal U.S. dollars, using midyear exchange rates to adjust EMIF Sur data denominated in non-U.S. currencies (e.g., pesos or quetzals).

Ranges of Estimates of Smuggling Revenues

We constructed a preliminary estimate, or range of estimates, of smuggling revenue from the low- and high-end figures for (1) unlawful migrant flows, (2) the percentage of those migrants who use smugglers, and (3) the migrants' payments to smugglers. First, we multiplied the low-end figures for each route, then we multiplied the high-end figures for each route, producing a low- and high-end estimate for each route. The DHS data yielded the low-end estimates, route by route, because they were lower for fees and the percentage of migrants using smugglers. At the high end, we were able to differentiate between payments en route to the U.S.-Mexico border as one "segment" of the journey and payments across that border as another "segment," because the EMIF Sur data on fees draw this distinction.

We found that the revenues from smuggling migrants from El Salvador, Guatemala, and Honduras, combined (as would correspond to the larger oval to the right in Figure S.1), could have ranged from a total of about $200 million to a total of about $2.3 billion in 2017 (see Table 3.1 in Chapter 3). The breadth of the range reflects the considerable uncertainty of the underlying estimates of unlawful migrant flows, migrants' use of smugglers, and smuggling fees. At the low end, this estimate very likely understates revenues, partly because of missing information on border crossings between POEs; at the high end, this estimate might be too high, partly because the fee data from EMIF Sur include agreed payments, some of which might not have materialized, in addition to actual payments.

However, neither end of the range includes fees from migrants who present themselves at POEs, which could increase the revenue estimates slightly, and neither end has been adjusted to account for recidivism, which could decrease them slightly (see Chapter 3).

Ranges of Estimates of Drug-Trafficking TCOs' Piso *Collections*

Separately, we developed an ancillary, preliminary estimate for drug-trafficking TCOs' tax, or *piso*, collections, using a similar methodology. The migrant flow numbers were the same as for the preliminary estimate of smuggling revenue, but the percentage and payment estimates differed substantially. Drawing on evidence from the literature review and discussion with SMEs, we postulated that the percentage of migrants who pay these taxes ranged from 50 percent to 75 percent and that the payment figures ranged from $300 to $700. On that basis, the total amount of *pisos* that migrants from the NT might have paid drug-trafficking TCOs in 2017—for traveling the three routes, combined (as would correspond to the smaller oval to the left in Figure S.1)—could have ranged from about $30 million to $180 million in 2017 (see Table 3.2 in Chapter 3).

Whether these sums are reflected in the human-smuggling revenues estimated above, as a pass through to drug-trafficking TCOs, or constitute an additional payment, depends on the smuggling arrangement, be it "all-inclusive" or "pay as you go." If the arrangement were all-inclusive, the tax might be folded into the smuggling fee (as depicted in the intersection of the two ovals in Figure S.1), but it would, nevertheless pass through to the drug-trafficking TCO that demanded payment for the migrant's passage. For this reason, and because of the attribution of the taxes to drug-trafficking TCOs, we present the estimate on its own.

Concluding Remarks

We developed a preliminary estimate of aggregate revenue from smuggling unlawful migrants from the NT to the United States that ranges from about $200 million to $2.3 billion in 2017. This estimate, as the range implies, is highly uncertain, owing largely to a scarcity of reliable data on migrant flows, migrants' use of smugglers, and smuggling fees. Likewise, we produced an ancillary and still preliminary estimate of drug-trafficking TCOs' tax, or *piso*, collections that also spanned an order of magnitude, from about $30 million to $180 million.

To conclude, we present implications of our findings for targeting human smuggling, informing resource allocation decisions, and improving data collection.

Targeting Human Smuggling

A key finding of this report is that human smuggling involves many different types of smugglers, or "actors," with organizations that are often informal and based on relationships instead of well-established, enduring hierarchies. Absent formality and strict hierarchical structures, it might be difficult for DHS to effectively target these actors with legal sanctions:

Loose networks are difficult to disrupt, ad hoc groups are even less susceptible to disruption, and independent operators are easily replaceable. Facilitators might be less replaceable than other market participants and present a more fruitful avenue for intervention, but going after them might be challenging, especially when they are based in foreign countries, as is typical. Although targeting might be difficult, DHS could consider expanding existing efforts to investigate payments made to human smugglers, especially in the United States, and working more closely with formal and informal banking services to identify suspicious payments. DHS could also consider expanding current efforts to work with foreign law enforcement partners.

Allocating Resources

As DHS considers how to allocate resources, it might look to compare the size of the human-smuggling market, as measured by estimated revenues, and the sizes of other illicit markets of concern. Our high-end estimate for revenue from human smuggling, i.e., $2.3 billion, was on the same order of magnitude as estimates for revenues from trafficking marijuana, cocaine, and heroin through Mexico and across the U.S.-Mexico border that were developed in a 2010 RAND report by Kilmer et al., which could have totaled up to $7.1 billion, without netting out the costs of the drugs. However, as noted above, we cannot say how much of the revenue from human smuggling flows to TCOs that engage in human smuggling. Moreover, the 2010 RAND estimates for drug-trafficking revenues include only revenues from moving drugs through Mexico and across the U.S.-Mexico border and do not include revenue that drug-trafficking TCOs garner subsequently from distribution, wholesale, or retail activities that occur in the United States. To shed additional light on the dimensions of human smuggling, we also compared revenues from human smuggling with spending on related licit activities, such as air, rail, truck, and other transportation services reported in national accounts, and, from that perspective, the smuggling revenues looked much smaller.

Improving Data Collection

We also identified potential improvements in data collection and methods that DHS could consider if it wanted to refine the estimate, to better inform policymaking. For example, DHS could standardize its line of questioning during migrant interviews, across apprehension sites, and seek details from migrants that would increase DHS's ability to assess revenues, by route, and distinguish different types of smugglers and payments. DHS could also create a shared portal for data entry that screens for errors, if it has not done so already, and use a randomized survey process to reduce the administrative burden of data collection on frontline personnel and increase the likelihood of successful data entry.

However, a longer-term research project might be able to reduce some of the uncertainty of the revenue estimate even using the imperfect data that DHS already has. For example, we could build on the calculations in this report by taking more time to explore the sensitivity of the calculations to underlying assumptions about behavior and markets and explore additional ways to filter and analyze the data.

Acknowledgments

We would like to thank John Vehmeyer for his work as our primary point of contact in the Science and Technology Directorate of the U.S. Department of Homeland Security (DHS) and Shawna Garrison, Advisor to the Commissioner for U.S. Customs and Border Protection, for her insight and assistance. In addition, we would like to thank the subject-matter experts within DHS—at U.S. Customs and Border Protection and U.S. Immigration and Customs Enforcement—and at academic institutions for their participation in interviews for this project. Because their participation was confidential, we cannot name them individually, but their contributions were critical to our understanding of the issues and the timely completion of the analysis. We would also like to thank Marc Rosenblum, Deputy Assistant Secretary for the Office of Immigration Statistics, for providing us with the DHS data that formed a large part of the analysis, and the Colegio de la Frontera Norte for publicly posting the data from its "Survey of Migration at Mexico's Southern Border" (EMIF Sur).

Lastly, we are grateful to several RAND colleagues, including Daniel Egel and Elina Treygor for their constructive feedback on earlier drafts of the report, Shelly Culberston for her contributions to the project design and interview protocol, Elizabeth Hammes for helping us conduct a rapid and wide-ranging literature review, Krista Romita Grocholski for her assistance with the data analysis, Holly Johnson for her support in formatting and preparing the report, James Torr for his thoughtful edits, and Erica Robles for her efforts to help us navigate Homeland Security Operational Analysis Center processes and meet challenging deadlines.

Abbreviations

DHS	U.S. Department of Homeland Security
EMIF Sur	Encuesta sobre Migración en la Frontera Sur de México/Survey of Migration at Mexico's Southern Border
HSOAC	Homeland Security Operational Analysis Center
POE	port of entry
NT	Northern Triangle (Guatemala, Honduras, and El Salvador)
SME	subject-matter expert
TCO	transnational criminal organization

1. Introduction

In 2017, U.S. Border Patrol agents apprehended about 160,000 unlawful migrants from the Northern Triangle (NT) of Central America—consisting of Guatemala, Honduras, and El Salvador—at the U.S.-Mexico border between ports of entry (POEs). An additional roughly 20,000 family units and unaccompanied children from these three countries presented themselves to U.S. Customs and Border Protection officers at POEs to enter the asylum process in 2017. Many or most of the migrants hired smugglers for assistance or paid others for rights of way at some point during the journey north. Migrants from the NT who hire smugglers might pay them thousands of dollars to make that journey, regardless of whether they attempt to evade capture or present themselves directly to border officials at or between POEs in order to claim asylum.[1] Figure 1.1 depicts common smuggling routes from NT countries through Mexico.

Figure 1.1. Smuggling Routes from the Northern Triangle to the United States

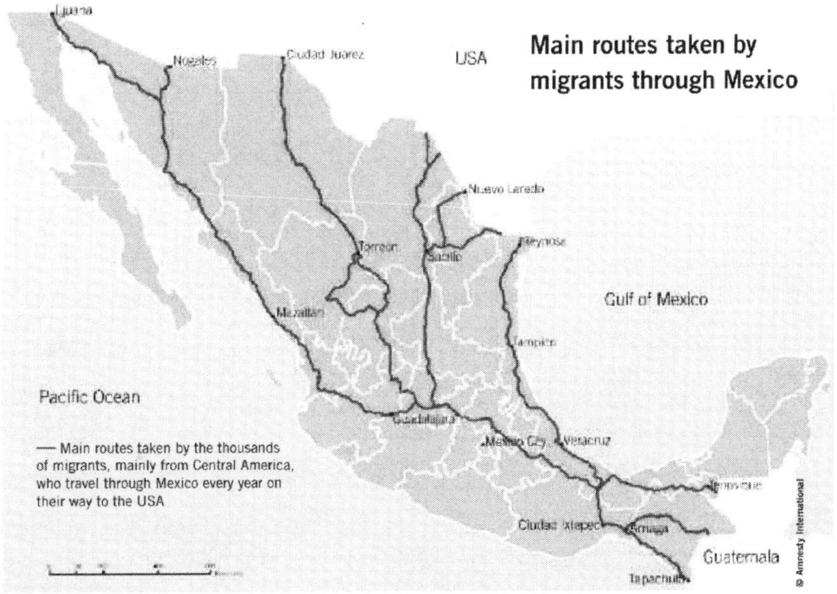

SOURCE: Amnesty International, 2010 (now CC BY-NC-ND 4.0).

Of particular concern to policymakers is the possibility that a substantial share of the migrants' expenditures on smuggling services is flowing to transnational criminal organizations

[1] In this context, we are using the term *border officials* to refer to U.S. Border Patrol agents *between* POEs and U.S. Customs and Border Protection officers *at* POEs because families and unaccompanied minors from the NT who use smugglers generally present themselves directly to agents and officers in both environments in order to enter the asylum process.

(TCOs). TCOs that benefit from smuggling migrants from the NT to the United States across the U.S.-Mexico border represent a potential threat to homeland security. They can create, contribute to, or help to shape a criminal industry that exploits and harms the people smuggled, challenges the rule of law in U.S. border states and the countries along transit routes, and degrades confidence in U.S. immigration laws.

To date, the U.S. Department of Homeland Security (DHS) and larger policy community have lacked evidence on the full extent and distribution of migrants' expenditures on smuggling and the characteristics of the smugglers, be they TCOs or others. Providing DHS with a better understanding of how TCOs and other actors that participate in human smuggling are structured, do business, and are financed could help inform efforts to investigate and disrupt them and to make decisions about how to allocate resources to those efforts. For example, such understanding could help DHS identify TCOs' vulnerabilities and supply evidence to weigh the benefits of action.

This report attempts to fill some of these knowledge gaps by presenting initial findings from a scoping study titled "Economic Value of Human Smuggling to Transnational Criminal Organizations." A primary goal of this study, which was conducted in less than two months, was to develop a preliminary estimate of TCOs' revenues from smuggling unlawful migrants from the NT to the United States. In addition, we sought to establish what is known or knowable about the characteristics, including the structure, operations, and financing, of TCOs that engage in human smuggling ("human-smuggling TCOs") along routes from the NT to the United States and the markets in which they operate.[2]

However, we encountered an immediate obstacle to meeting the study's research goals, particularly those of revenue estimation. We found, by interviewing subject-matter experts (SMEs), reviewing the literature, and analyzing data, that many different types of smugglers participate in this market and that we could not credibly distinguish the activities and revenues of human-smuggling TCOs from those of independent operators, ad hoc groups, and others who also benefit from human smuggling. Thus, we could not consider the characteristics of human-smuggling TCOs in isolation nor could we provide an estimate, or even a range of estimates, for revenues flowing solely to human-smuggling TCOs. Instead, we developed a range for revenues that flow to all types of human smugglers, including TCOs. We were, however, able to attribute the revenues from taxes levied on migrants by drug-trafficking TCOs on portions of routes they control directly to those TCOs and estimate them separately.

---

[2] Notwithstanding the focus on revenue as a starting point for understanding "economic value," profitability might say more about human smuggling's contribution to the financial health and viability of these TCOs.

Definition of *Transnational Criminal Organization*

To start, we examined formal definitions of *transnational criminal organization* to try to distinguish such organizations from others that might engage in human smuggling along routes from the NT to the United States. TCOs have been defined in U.S. law as

> . . . self-perpetuating associations who operate transnationally for the purpose of obtaining power, influence, monetary and/or commercial gains, wholly or in part by illegal means, while protecting their activities through a pattern of corruption and/or violence, or while protecting their illegal activities through a transnational organizational structure and the exploitation of transnational commerce or communication mechanisms.[3]

The White House's 2011 *Strategy to Combat Transnational Organized Crime* provides further guidance:

> There is no single structure under which transnational organized criminals operate; they vary from hierarchies to clans, networks, and cells, and may evolve to other structures. The crimes they commit also vary. Transnational organized criminals act conspiratorially in their criminal activities and possess certain characteristics which may include, but are not limited to:
>
> - In at least part of their activities they commit violence or other acts which are likely to intimidate, or make actual or implicit threats to do so;
> - They exploit differences between countries to further their objectives, enriching their organization, expanding its power, and/or avoiding detection/apprehension;
> - They attempt to gain influence in government, politics, and commerce through corrupt as well as legitimate means;
> - They have economic gain as their primary goal, not only from patently illegal activities but also from investment in legitimate businesses; and
> - They attempt to insulate both their leadership and membership from detection, sanction, and/or prosecution through their organizational structure.[4]

These definitions and guidance allow for different types of organizational structures, ranging from hierarchies to cells, but they start from the point of "self-perpetuating associations" that act

---

[3] 10 U.S.C. § 284(i)(6). For an alternative definition, see United Nations Office on Drugs and Crime, *Legislative Guide for the Implementation of the United Nations Convention Against Transnational Organized Crime*, 2004. For the purposes of that convention, the United Nations specifies,

> (a) "Organized criminal group" shall mean a structured group of three or more persons, existing for a period of time and acting in concert with the aim of committing one or more serious crimes or offences established in accordance with this Convention, in order to obtain, directly or indirectly, a financial or other material benefit; (b) "Serious crime" shall mean conduct constituting an offence punishable by a maximum deprivation of liberty of at least four years or a more serious penalty; (c) "Structured group" shall mean a group that is not randomly formed for the immediate commission of an offence and that does not need to have formally defined roles for its members, continuity of its membership or a developed structure.

[4] United States, Executive Office of the President, 2011.

like organizations and call out particular behavior, including violence in pursuit of influence and economic gain. These descriptions suggest that, to be considered a TCO, a human-smuggling group or network needs to have some level of organization and hierarchy; that is, it should be more than just an ad hoc collection of individuals who operate along distinct parts of a route and work together opportunistically with other individuals in various configurations to move people from Central America, across Mexico, and to the U.S. border. One gray area involves slightly more organized groups, consisting of loose networks of individuals who consistently work together or generally leverage the same set of connections along a route.

As Chapter 2 shows, our review of the literature and interviews with SMEs suggest that smugglers bringing migrants from the NT to the U.S. border fall along a spectrum from independent operators, to ad hoc groups of individuals, to loose networks, and to more-formal networks that consistently work together—and it is possible that the same actor may be engaging in human smuggling in some or all of those ways at any given time. This means that even with a formal, official definition, the lines between TCOs and other kinds of smugglers and smuggling networks are blurry. These blurry lines presented substantial analytical challenges and contributed to the difficulty of determining whether migrants are hiring TCOs to smuggle them along a route and how much they are paying them.

Technical Approach to Analysis

Given the short time frame for this study, we turned to existing literature, available data, and SMEs to learn more about the characteristics of human-smuggling TCOs and other actors that engage in human smuggling:

- **We reviewed existing literature** related, for example, to the types of TCOs that engage in human smuggling along routes from the NT, the flows of migrants from the NT to the United States, the fees that migrants pay to smugglers, and the costs of smuggling.[5]
- **We reviewed available DHS and other data** to cast light on the structure, operations, and financing of TCOs and support revenue estimation, including data on migration flows, smuggling fees, and smugglers' costs.
- **We reached out to SMEs,** including U.S. government officials and academics, to gain their perspectives on this topic and to learn more about available documentation and data. (See Appendix B for more details.)

With this evidence, we implemented a multimethod analysis: We developed a qualitative narrative (see Chapter 2) and scoped the market for smuggling services quantitatively (see Chapter 3). The distinction between the approaches as "quantitative" and "qualitative" is not clear-cut; for example, for our narrative we drew on anecdotal quantitative evidence, culled from

---

[5] Our literature review included academic articles, press reports, and reports written by government agencies, non-governmental organizations, and multilateral entities. See Appendix A for more details.

the literature, and for the scoping exercise we drew partly from qualitative survey data. By "triangulating" among methods and evidence, we could characterize the TCOs and other entities that engage in human smuggling and set out a general analytical framework for conceptualizing and addressing revenue estimation.

Our study framework, shown in Figure 1.2, depicts a generic, stylized route that begins at a point of origin in the NT, continues through Mexico, and ends at a destination in the United States, given the possibilities that a route can consist of multiple segments, that not all smugglers are TCOs, that not all unlawful migrants hire smugglers of any type for all segments, and various other route characteristics. The route characteristics suggest the kinds of data that would be necessary to conduct an economic analysis, including revenue estimation. The characteristics depicted in Figure 1.2 consist of the route segment, types of smugglers (e.g., TCO, other, or self), smuggling fees, other migrant payments, costs to smugglers, and the number of migrants along the route who travel under those conditions.

Figure 1.2. General Framework for Economic Analysis, Including Revenue Estimation

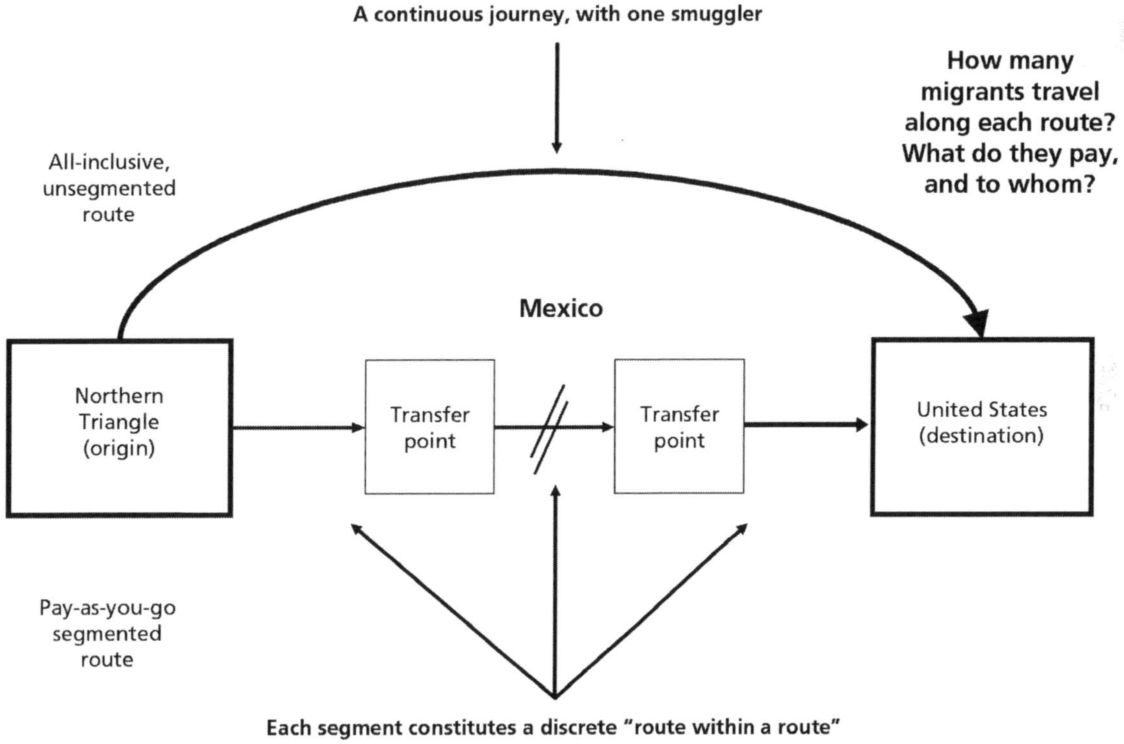

NOTES: Hash lines along the segmented route suggest the potential for more segments.

Some of these characteristics could be parsed further; for example, "other payments" could be divided into bribes to officials and taxes, or *pisos*, that drug-trafficking TCOs levy along the routes they control. These bribes and taxes might or might not be included in smuggling fees, as a pass through, depending on the particulars of the smuggling arrangement.[6]

Although not apparent in Figure 1.2, we confined our analysis to a recent period, mostly 2015–2017, and to unlawful migrants coming from and originating in NT countries. As addressed below and in later chapters of this report, data on important elements of the framework were lacking, which substantially hindered progress on revenue estimation, even as a range, and generated considerable uncertainty.[7]

Challenges, Uncertainties, and Mitigations

We faced analytical challenges relating to time constraints and data quality, completeness, and relevance that yielded a high degree of uncertainty about the findings, especially those concerning revenues.

To mitigate the challenges of an abbreviated timeline (less than two months for the evidence collection, analysis, and writing), we "triangulated," as noted above; independently analyzed the data that we obtained from DHS and other sources; and cross-checked our results with those of other researchers who have worked with similar and different data sets to identify and understand apparent divergences. In addition, as addressed below, we set out to frame our preliminary estimates of revenue, including embedded calculations of unlawful migrant flows, smuggling fees, etc., in terms of ranges. Lastly, we also considered options for improving the fidelity of our estimates under less-binding time constraints.

The data-related challenges were at least as noteworthy.

The data on unlawful migration and human smuggling—like any data on illicit activities—tend to be partial, unreliable, and sometimes ill-suited to the policy questions at hand. Some data derive from direct observation (i.e., the number of individuals that U.S. Border Patrol agents apprehend, see turning back, or see getting away), some derive from statistical analysis that extrapolates from current trends (e.g., migrant flow–estimation methodologies related to recidivism rates), and others derive from surveys of or interviews with migrants and smugglers. All of them have limitations, which are discussed in Chapter 3.

Inevitably, researchers must also grapple with what criminologists call the "dark figure," referring to the amount of unreported or undiscovered illicit activity. For human smuggling, this gap in the data could pertain both to the activities of smugglers and to the flows of unlawful migrants from the NT to the United States. For example, law enforcement is unlikely to observe or understand the totality of a TCO's operations, partly because TCOs seek to conceal them and also because individuals who are affiliated with TCOs may not divulge this information upon

---

[6] Chapter 2 includes a detailed discussion of migrants' payments of taxes, or *pisos*, to TCOs, specifically drug-trafficking TCOs, and Chapter 3 provides an ancillary preliminary estimate of their worth.

[7] For more information about the estimation method, see Chapter 3 and Appendix C.

capture. Indeed, some or even most people working for a TCO may have little knowledge of the TCO's overall activity. Similarly, government officials will not see all individuals who turn back or get away, and migrants may not provide full information about their journeys. Smuggling, like other illicit activities, tends to rely on trust relationships, and disclosures would violate that trust, risking reprisals and denials of service in the future.

Moreover, researchers cannot presume the accuracy of data related to smuggling or migration. For example, U.S. Border Patrol agents often interview migrants and ask them questions about the details of their journeys, such as smuggling fees, and record the results. However, these officials might ask these questions differently at different locations and might misinterpret or mis-enter the results and migrants might answer these questions incorrectly, either purposefully or because they did not understand the questions.[8]

In addition, as noted above, not all human smugglers are affiliated with TCOs, howsoever defined, and the data provide little insight as to whether migrants hire human-smuggling TCOs or other types of actors. To the best of our knowledge, neither DHS nor any other agency or academic researcher has collected data on smuggling fees that specify smuggler "type" or provide information that could tie the DHS data on smuggling fees to data on smugglers' organizational affiliations. Thus, even if we could distinguish clearly between human-smuggling TCOs and other types of smugglers, and even if we could also develop a reliable estimate of revenues from smuggling NT migrants to the United States, we could not parse the revenues to those TCOs, specifically.

Lastly, estimating revenue from human smuggling, as compared with drug trafficking, presents other challenges relating both to the diversity of the individuals seeking to be smuggled and to the diversity of smuggling services being offered. Drugs are relatively simple, near-homogeneous commodities, and trafficking them involves commensurately little differentiation. A kilogram of cocaine is a kilogram of cocaine, after some adjustment for purity, and trafficking involves moving that kilogram from one place to another, with limited options, e.g., regarding routes and modes of transportation.[9] By contrast, people differ widely—e.g., by gender, age, health status, and physical capability—as do their needs and financial resources. Consequently, human smugglers can differentiate their services, with options including comprehensive "all-inclusive" or "end-to-end" packages on one end of the spectrum, and "pay-as-you go" arrangements, in which migrants pay for discrete services, at the other. (See Chapter 2.) As a result, smuggling fees can and do vary greatly from one journey to another.

None of these challenges has a fully satisfying "fix." For example, to estimate migrant flows, researchers have developed methods based largely on data on apprehensions of unlawful

---

[8] For more information about specific shortcomings of the data, see Chapter 3.

[9] See, for example, Paoli, Greenfield, and Zoutendijk, 2013. For more on drug supply chains, see also Paoli and Greenfield, 2017.

migrants. These results may be biased upward or downward, depending on the approach, and some of them may be controversial, but they can be and are used to estimate ranges.[10] Regarding the revenues and profits associated with human smuggling, one researcher asks whether it is even possible to conduct economic analyses of this market, because the activity is illegal and highly differentiated.[11] Notwithstanding the "dark figure," other researchers have found ways to deal with illegality in more homogeneous markets, but the diversity of services in this arena would add a layer of complexity.[12]

Some of the least "fixable" challenges are among those most closely aligned with the primary goal of the study: revenue estimation. From the start, we recognized the infeasibility of developing a point estimate for smuggling revenues and intended, instead, to frame any revenue estimate as a range, from low to high, because of the time constraint and also to accommodate the considerable uncertainty in the data. Furthermore, as the research progressed, we found that we lacked an empirical basis for separating the activities and revenues of human-smuggling TCOs from those of others, including ad hoc groups and independent operators, who engage in human smuggling. Thus, we could provide, at best, a range for revenues to all smugglers, irrespective of their affiliations, although we were able to provide a separate preliminary estimate of the right-of-way taxes that migrants pay to drug-trafficking TCOs.

The following chapter presents initial findings on the characteristics of human smugglers that operate along routes from the NT to the United States, as well as the characteristics of human smuggling, more generally, with a focus on actors' roles and the services they provide.

---

[10] See, for example, DHS, Office of Immigration Statistics, 2017.

[11] See Sanchez, 2017, 2018.

[12] Reuter and Greenfield, 2001; Paoli, Greenfield, and Reuter, 2009.

2. The Characteristics of Human Smuggling

This chapter focuses on the characteristics of human smuggling from the NT countries (Guatemala, Honduras, and El Salvador) to the United States, including the structure, operations, and financing of human smugglers. We provide an overview of the main types of smugglers, or "actors," that engage in this market, analyze the roles they typically fill, and discuss the services such actors provide, the fees they charge for those services, and the costs they incur. In effect, this chapter covers the "who," "what," "how," and financial dimensions of human smuggling along routes from the NT to the United States. We conclude the chapter by exploring the linkages between human smuggling and drug-trafficking TCOs.

Smugglers that move migrants from the NT to the United States take many forms, only some of which appear to meet the definition of *transnational criminal organization* laid out in U.S. law and policy guidance, as discussed in Chapter 1. While most unlawful migrants report having engaged the services of a smuggler for at least a portion of the route, it is unclear how many migrants engage smugglers to arrange their entire journey north or engage smugglers for discrete portions of the journey, and how many are using more-organized TCO-like networks as compared with independent operators and ad hoc groups.

The routes migrants use to travel north are well established and primarily follow overland transportation corridors from the NT to Mexico's southern border with Guatemala, and then up through Mexico to the border with the United States. The main variation appears to involve the modes of transportation or conveyances that migrants use, which include buses, taxis, tractor trailers, and freight trains, with comparatively few NT migrants using sea vessels or airplanes for parts of the journey.

Fees paid by unlawful migrants also differ widely, depending on the comprehensiveness and quality of smuggling services that migrants engage. Some migrants can pay thousands of dollars to be smuggled from their home country to the interior of the United States, while others may only pay a few hundred dollars for discrete portions of their journey. Migrants often pay taxes, or *pisos*, to drug-trafficking TCOs (or "cartels") to travel through territory the cartels control, and bribes to officials to go through checkpoints along the routes. Such payments might be in addition to other smuggling fees or included in them, depending on the particular arrangements that migrants make with their smugglers. Migrants' payments to drug-trafficking TCOs are not payments for smuggling, per se, but they are the only revenue associated with human smuggling that we could attribute directly to TCOs of some kind.

Lastly, while the scope of this report is limited to migrants from the NT, our literature review and SME interviews suggest that the smuggling groups operating along this corridor are also moving people of other nationalities. The evidence suggests that these migrants—particularly those from countries outside the Western Hemisphere—may be paying smuggling fees that are orders of magnitude higher. Additionally, the groups specializing in facilitating this extra-hemispheric flow may be more organized and, thus, potentially more liable to meet the definition of a TCO.

Taxonomy of Human Smugglers

Different types of actors participate in human smuggling, including independent operators that move migrants along particular segments of the route or offer other discrete services (for example, a taxi driver based out of one town on the route that ferries migrants to the next major town); ad hoc or opportunistic groups that might work together from time to time but not regularly; and more-formal enterprises or networks.[13] This reality means that migrants who intend to travel to the United States from Central America can choose from a wide range of service options. At one end of the spectrum, migrants can opt for "all-inclusive" or "end-to-end" arrangements, whereby they pay one facilitator, group, or network that arranges all their travel and may even send a representative to travel with them; at the other end, migrants can "pay as they go," traveling on their own for parts of the route and connecting with local smugglers to pay for transportation and logistical support for other parts of the route. The differences in the kinds of services that are provided by these actors are discussed in more detail below.

There is some debate in the literature about the extent to which groups of smugglers are becoming more professional and sophisticated, in light of possible increases in smuggling fees.[14] However, the majority of sources suggest that most of these groups are loosely organized, are nonhierarchical, and do not maintain a definable command structure.[15] The diversity and proliferation of individuals and groups involved in some aspect of human smuggling make it challenging to identify the extent to which these activities are conducted by actual TCOs.

As noted in Chapter 1, the statutory definition of a TCO includes components that do not appear to be present in many human-smuggling operations, including TCOs being "self-perpetuating associations" that protect their activities through "a pattern of corruption and/or violence," with a "transnational organizational structure."[16]

Table 2.1 presents a taxonomy of human smugglers, based on our review of the literature and interviews with SMEs, starting with the least organized types of smugglers and ending with the most organized. At each level, actors differ by organizational cohesion, membership, and

---

[13] See, for example, Guevara González, 2018.

[14] For a discussion of debate among academic sources on organizational coherence of smuggling organizations, see Sanchez and Zhang, 2018.

[15] Sanchez, 2017, p. 14; Zhang, 2007, p. 89; Guevara González, 2018, pp. 180–184. For example, "A key feature of the smuggling strategy along the U.S.-Mexico border is its relatively low entry costs and lack of vertical integration" (Wuebbels, 2004, p. 23).

[16] 10 U.S.C. § 284.

geographic dispersion along smuggling corridors. The more organized networks can feature transnational organizational structures, but relatively few appear to meet the bar of being "self-perpetuating associations." And while many of these actors rely on corruption to protect their activities in the form of bribes to officials, relatively few of them appear to use violence for this purpose. The taxonomy should be thought of as a spectrum rather than a set of firm categories; smugglers commonly move between levels or can operate at more than one level along the spectrum, depending on their opportunities. Many of these actors, even those toward the more organized end of the spectrum, can function as subcontractors to other actors at the same or different levels of the spectrum.

Table 2.1. The Spectrum of Actors Engaged in Human Smuggling

Type of Actor	Organizational Structure	Services	Group Membership	Geographic Reach
Independent operators	One "cell" composed of one or a few individuals	Provide a discrete service (e.g., transportation or lodging)	Do not generally work with other cells or actors	Generally work in one location, or between two locations
Ad hoc groups	Two or more independent operators that may not always work together	Provide multiple, complementary services	Generally unaware of other actors and groups more than one degree of separation removed	Work in one, two, or more locations
Loose networks	A larger number of small groups that usually work together	May provide end-to-end service along the full route or a portion of the route	Members may only know a limited number of other members	Working in many locations, potentially the full route
More-formal networks	A central figure who coordinates groups that consistently work together	Provide end-to-end services	Members generally know each other	Working along the full route

Independent Operators

Smuggling services are often provided by local, independent operators who generally operate in one area and facilitate the movement of migrants along discrete sections of the route from Central America to the U.S. border.[17] These services can include providing facilitation, transportation, housing, food, and fraudulent documents.[18] For example, there may be a "transportation cell," or a small group of individuals, in Tapachula that specializes in recruiting recently arrived migrants from the bus station or border and transporting them to the next major

[17] Sanchez, 2018.

[18] For example, "Martinez appears to be an independent contractor. He said he charges $2,500 for the trip from the Guatemalan border to the U.S. border, where he gives Central American migrants fake Mexican identity cards and makes them learn the first stanza of the Mexican national anthem before handing them off to another smuggler" (Associated Press, 2014).

waypoint along the route north.[19] This group may not have any formal connections to other smuggling groups, instead focusing solely on moving migrants that it encounters or recruits from one city to the next one.[20]

Ad Hoc Groups

Sometimes, several generally independent operators may come together to pool their services for a given migrant or group of migrants.[21] These opportunistic or ad hoc groupings of smugglers are generally not stable or allegiant to each other, and the smugglers may be working with several different groups at the same time. Expanding on the previous example, the transportation cell in Tapachula may know several different operators that provide housing in the next major waypoint for migrants, and the cell will put its clients in contact with one of them. The group that provides housing might essentially direct migrants to a low-grade hotel (also known as a "stash house") that takes in migrants from other organizations operating along that segment of the route. The stash house operator, in turn, might then connect the migrants with another transportation cell that the migrants would use for the next portion of their journey. The two transportation cells may not be aware of each other, even though both cells participated in smuggling the same migrants along the route.

Loose Networks

Some smuggling networks along the routes consist of groups that might not be attached formally and consistently to one organization—that is, they might not answer uniformly to the same person—but that generally work with the same preferred or trusted partners along longer sections of the route.[22] These loose networks generally work together, and in some cases the chain of facilitation can extend all the way from the NT to the United States, although the links in the chain might not all know or be aware of each other. The main difference between these loose networks and the ad hoc groupings is that these networks are more organized and the

---

[19] In an interview with PBS Frontline, a smuggler operating as an independent operator admits to finding clients at a bus stop where recently unlawful migrants who have been removed are released (Frontline/World, 2018).

[20] See, for example, Sanchez, 2018; Zhang, 2007; Campana, 2016; Associated Press, 2014.

[21] See, for example, this description of how unlawful migrants arriving at a town on the Guatemala border with Mexico are connected with smugglers:

> As migrants arrive into town, they are approached by taxi drivers who offer their transportation services. Drivers recommend specific hotels or accommodations to their customers, receiving in turn a commission based on the amount of business they bring in. Hotels also serve as brokerage points for those who arrive without a guide. Once at a hotel, migrants in transit can select from a vast range of options, including accommodations, meals, transportation toward the border with Mexico, and assistance crossing the southern border for a fee. (Guevara González, 2018).

[22] See, for example, a Mexican news magazine's description of how three coyotes coordinate the travel of El Salvadorans to Houston (Martinez, 2017).

various components of the network along the route tend to work together consistently, even if one person does not manage the overall network.[23] An example of this kind of network would involve a facilitator in Guatemala who recruits migrants and then tasks another individual or group with transporting the migrant to the border with Mexico, where yet another individual or group would take custody of the migrant and be responsible for transporting the migrant further north.[24] The migrant may be handed off several times along the trip, with the facilitator being generally aware of the migrant's progress, but the groups that transport and provide housing to the migrant may only be loosely aware of each other.

More-Formal Networks

Formal, relatively more-hierarchical smuggling networks reportedly exist along the routes from Central America to the United States.[25] However, even these relatively more-organized groups feature command structures that are not truly hierarchical, particularly compared with other organized crime actors, such as cartels or drug-trafficking TCOs. For example, one individual might not have command and control over all of their affiliates or subsidiaries. These relatively more-formal networks generally feature one person or a group of persons that oversees the activities of others in the network, and these networks usually offer "all-inclusive" packages, whereby migrants pay a substantial fee for end-to-end service all the way from their point of origin to their destination in the United States. Some of these networks also appear to specialize in moving migrants from outside the Western Hemisphere.[26]

Dynamism Within the Spectrum

Low barriers to entry, opportunistic behavior, and fluid allegiances suggest dynamism within the spectrum and make it difficult to reliably assign smugglers—including, individuals, cells, or even some groups—to particular parts of the spectrum. Even if would-be smugglers must have some risk tolerance, many of the activities they engage in do not require specialized knowledge (e.g., driving a taxi, operating a hotel or stash house), such that individuals, in particular, can

---

[23] See, for example, the hierarchy of human-smuggling groups in Palacios's (2014) academic article from less to more organized, culminating with "Systematic complex networks are more extensive and have a hierarchical structure in which a leader manages the network's business and finances" (p. 327).

[24] See, for example, Martinez, 2017.

[25] See, for example, the description of human-smuggling networks in Associated Press (2014) as "a complex corporate structure. Guides at the border usually work for honchos who run the operation from afar and only pocket a fraction of the price charged to the migrants. One of the most important coyotes moving immigrants from El Salvador lives in Texas."

[26] See, for example, U.S. Immigration and Customs Enforcement, 2016.

come and go easily.[27] Additionally, at any point in time a smuggler might be operating independently, as a member of an ad hoc group, and as a member of a loose network. That is to say, the coalitions of smugglers that operate along the routes from Central America to the United States are opportunistic, extremely fluid, and prone to change, making it extremely difficult to pin down the exact nature of smuggling or of specific groups and networks that are involved in the trade. As noted above and described in the taxonomy, only some actors appear to meet the definition of *transnational criminal organization* found in U.S. law and policy guidance.

Key Roles in Human Smuggling

Smugglers typically fill a number of roles, whether they are working as independent operators or as part of a network or group. Depending on the sophistication of the operation, individuals or small groups of people (sometimes referred to as a *cell* by law enforcement) can fill these roles.[28] Some of these individuals and cells work as subcontractors or independent operators and may offer their services to several different networks or other smugglers at the same time. This means that human-smuggling networks may feature several cells that work together occasionally or consistently, depending on the relative strength of the networks.

The following is a brief description of the key roles:[29]

- **Facilitation/coordination.** Identify and recruit migrants, collect up-front fees, pay other smuggling organizations during the migrant's journey, and coordinate some or all of the migrants' travel from their source country to their final destination. These individuals or small groups are often based in the NT countries, though some might also be present in population centers in Mexico.[30]
- **Transportation.** Transport migrants from one location to another along the route north. Transportation involves conveyances of different types and sophistication, with actors and modes ranging from local taxi drivers that transport small numbers of migrants from one town to another, to organizations that charter buses or retain tractor trailers to transport large groups long distances. Part of this service often includes paying fees or taxes, including bribes and *pisos* (see the later discussion), to other criminal networks or corrupt officials to cross their territory or pass a checkpoint.

---

[27] For example, Guevara González (2018) describes an interview with a woman who recounts that the first two times she journeyed north, she used smugglers: "By her third trip, she felt confident enough to travel on her own—and now she puts her experience to work facilitating the journeys of unlawful migrants through Mexico."

[28] For further discussion of the unique roles of participants of smuggling organizations, see United Nations Office on Drugs and Crime, 2011, p. 70.

[29] As noted earlier, Guevara González (2018) explains how many of these functions work along the border between Guatemala and Mexico.

[30] See, for example, Garsd's (2016) interview with a smuggler based in Mexico who describes how his network coordinates a series of "walkers" to help Honduran migrants traverse Mexico to the border with the United States.

- **Logistics/stash houses.** Provide logistical support, often in the form of lodging or stash houses where migrants can take shelter for a few days or even a few weeks. On the U.S. side of the border, stash house operators often move migrants between houses every few days to attract less attention from neighbors and law enforcement.[31]
- **Fraudulent documents.** Provide fraudulent documents for unlawful migrants, such as Mexican visas, national identity cards, and birth certificates. These documents can help migrants travel freely through Mexico and, in some cases, can also be used to create evidence of "synthetic families" with unaccompanied children to present to border officials upon entry into the United States.[32]
- **Footguides/coyotes/*polleros*.** Guide unlawful migrants—generally single adults—on foot across the land border between POEs, to avoid detection by U.S. Border Patrol agents while entering the United States. These footguides are commonly known as *coyotes* or *polleros*. The term *coyote* is also used interchangeably to describe human smugglers in general, and some reports note that these more broadly defined coyotes may operate in the NT countries, travel with migrants throughout their journey, and operate along the U.S.-Mexico border.[33] At the border, footguides often work in concert with "spotters" who try to locate law enforcement assets and personnel to maneuver groups around them via radio or cell phone.

The Relationship Between Smuggling Services and Fees

Human smugglers provide migrants with a wide range of services, including transportation, lodging, and specialized knowledge to help migrants avoid arrest, extortion, and violence by evading detection or paying bribes and protection fees. Migrants can choose to "pay as they go" and find the services they need for discrete sections of the route north (which may cost them very little in fees), or use "all-inclusive" or "end-to-end" packages that cover their travel from their point of origin to their final destination in the United States (such packages, by comparison, may cost them more than $10,000).[34] We were unable to find much evidence in the literature on how many unlawful migrants are using all-inclusive arrangements versus choosing to pay as they go. Smugglers' services can differ widely based on the needs and financial resources of their clients and, consequently, so can their fees.

All-Inclusive Packages

Our review of the literature revealed substantial variation in the fees that smugglers charge for all-inclusive services, but there appears to be broad convergence around these kinds of

---

[31] For example, Nixon and Heisler (2018) describe the key role stash houses play in smuggling migrants in Texas.

[32] For example, Castellano (2014) reports how smugglers in Guatemala describe their connections with Mexican immigration authorities and their ability to procure visas to facilitate travel through Mexico, and Hennessy-Fiske (2018) reports on unrelated adults and children posing as families at the border.

[33] See Martinez's (2017) discussion of the three coyotes involved in smuggling migrants from the NT to Houston.

[34] Sanchez, 2018.

services costing migrants between $6,000 and $10,000, which is roughly in line with the results of the Encuesta sobre Migración en la Frontera Sur de México, or Survey of Migration at Mexico's Southern Border (which we refer to by its Spanish abbreviation, EMIF Sur), conducted at the Mexico-Guatemala border by the Colegio de la Frontera Norte, located in Mexico. However, some articles suggest that the fees can be substantially higher. There is also evidence that the fees can vary, depending on whether unlawful migrants are attempting to evade detection at the border, and thus must be smuggled into the interior of the United States (generally single adults), or whether they are turning themselves into border officials at and between POEs and entering the asylum process (generally families and unaccompanied children).[35]

Smugglers can also provide specialized services for clients such as children, pregnant women, and the elderly that reduce exposure to risks and do not require extensive physical activity, such as scaling walls or extended hikes through remote terrain.[36] As one smuggler explains, specialized services that increase a person's chances of successfully evading detection, such as the use of decoys, lookouts, and safe houses, are likely to drive up costs and therefore prices.[37] Some reporting also suggests that smugglers can charge exorbitant fees if they have access to corrupt customs officials who take bribes in exchange for "looking the other way" as migrants' pass through borders.[38] Alternatively, migrants of greater means may choose transportation methods that are more comfortable, such as taxis or personal vehicles, or pay additional fees for smuggling tactics that minimize the risk of detection, such as using fraudulent travel documents. As one scholar notes, "the more money you have, the better service you get."[39]

Selected examples of smuggling fees in press reports are broadly representative:

- A 2018 *New York Times* article drawing on interviews with unlawful migrants found that the fee to enter the United States illegally represented more than half of the overall fee of $12,500 that a family paid for one individual's journey: "The nearly 2,000-mile trip had already cost Mr. Cruz's family more than $6,000 and brought him within sight of Brownsville, Tex. The remaining 500 miles to Houston—terrain prowled by the United States Border Patrol as well as the state and local police—would set them back another $6,500."[40]

---

[35] See, for example, Martinez's (2017) description of the *viaje corto*, or short journey, taken by asylum seekers that allows them to avoid paying the extra fees to avoid detection. Miroff (2018) describes the increasing trend of migrants turning themselves in to border officials. For additional reporting on fees and cost, see *Daily Mail* and Associated Press Reporters, 2014, and Kulish, 2018.

[36] Sanchez, 2017.

[37] González and Solis, 2017.

[38] Frontline/World, 2018.

[39] Cleek, 2018.

[40] Kulish, 2018.

- A Public Radio International news segment in 2018 described smuggling fees doubling over the past decade: "But in the past few years, the price of this trip has skyrocketed to between $7,000 and $10,000, more than double what it was a decade ago."[41]
- A Mexican online magazine interviewed a smuggler specializing in bringing unlawful migrants from El Salvador to the United States who described how he had raised his fees in 2017 after increased enforcement. The smuggler noted that he used to charge around $8,000 for travel from El Salvador to Houston, but he was now charging $9,500 to $10,000—plus another $1,500 if the unlawful migrants wanted to go past Houston.[42]
- During a National Public Radio interview in 2016, a smuggler claimed to charge as much as $17,000–$19,000 during the interview, while the director of a nonprofit working with unlawful migrants cited a lower figure: "You have to assume the average price is between 6,000 and 10,000. If you pay more, you're more likely to get through without being detected."[43]
- An academic researcher who volunteered at a migrant shelter along the Mexico-Guatemala border during parts of 2014, 2015, and 2016 noted: "Coyotes are known for providing a full-service package, which includes the facilitation of journeys across Mexico and into specific destinations within the United States from the place of origin or residence of the migrant. Few migrants travel in this all-inclusive way, though, because of cost: coyote-led door-to-door journeys are quite expensive. During the period in which this research was carried out, the prices of such all-inclusive packages ranged between 4,000 and 6,000 U.S. dollars."[44]
- An article detailed negotiations with several smugglers in Guatemala in 2014; loosely translated, it stated: "Besides 'The Chuluyo' we negotiated separately with three more Guatemalan traffickers to move 'Karen.' The cost ranged from 6,000–9,000 dollars, with two to three attempts to achieve it." [45]
- An Associated Press article in 2014 included interviews with smugglers: "The trafficker on the Guatemalan border, who spoke with The Associated Press after an intermediary negotiated the time and place, said the people he smuggles pay $10,000 a head for the trip from Central America, which covers everything from hotel and train payments to official bribes and cartel taxes. But occasionally, he said, a cartel will demand as much as an extra $5,000 on threat of death."[46]

These reports generally do not, however, shed light on another key research question: What percentage of unlawful migrants are opting to pay for these "all-inclusive" packages? One exception is an investigative report by the Mexican newspaper *El Universal* into human smuggling from Guatemala, which noted that 75 percent of unaccompanied children hired a

---

[41] Cleek, 2018.

[42] Martinez, 2017.

[43] Garsd, 2018.

[44] Guevara González, 2018, p. 182.

[45] Castellano, 2014.

[46] Associated Press, 2014.

smuggling network and were accompanied by representatives of these networks—"coyotes"—during their entire journey.[47]

Pay-as-You-Go Arrangements

An unknown percentage of unlawful migrants choose to travel on their own without engaging a smuggler to coordinate their entire journey. Instead, they obtain services, as needed, along the route. During their journey, they can enter into agreements with multiple facilitators at different stages in their journeys north, each of which might offer different level of services, possibly tailored to their needs and resources, a model often described as "pay-as-you-go."[48] Because the arrangements are spontaneous, we were unable to find many estimates of what unlawful migrants pay for these discrete services.

One researcher who spent time living in a shelter, known as "La 72," catering to unlawful migrants along Mexico's border with Guatemala noted that "Most Central American migrants staying at La 72 reported relying on the segmented facilitation, where they relied on a guide (*guía* in Spanish) to lead them through specific portions of their journeys. *Guías* are typically local residents . . . with knowledge of the terrain."[49] The researcher went on to describe how unlawful migrants arriving at the town are approached by taxi drivers who offer them transportation and connect them with other logistics providers in the town, who in turn can connect them with a wide array of other services.[50] The fees charged to migrants for segmented facilitation varied significantly, but some of the prices she observed being negotiated for discrete services included

- $15 per night for a bed in a shared hotel room
- $1–$4 to cross the river in a boat
- $1,000 for a guaranteed crossing of the Mexico-Guatemala border past immigration checkpoints on the Mexican side.[51]

In another example, a *New York Times* reporter followed the travels of an unlawful migrant from El Salvador whose family in the United States wired money at different points in the journey when he was unable to continue on his own—including a substantial payment at the beginning of his travel: "Just two days into Mr. Cruz's journey, his family had to wire the smuggling network $1,900 to get him through southern Mexico."[52]

---

[47] Castellano, 2014.

[48] Sanchez, 2018; Organisation for Economic Co-operation and Development, 2015.

[49] Guevara González, 2018, p. 182.

[50] Guevara González, 2018, p. 183.

[51] Guevara González, 2018, pp. 183–187.

[52] Kulish, 2018.

In yet another example, experts interviewed by Public Radio International described the range of options available to unlawful migrants who set out on their own: "Migrants who have no money can hitchhike, walk or take the train. . . . Some families pay smugglers a few hundred dollars to explain the route. . . . With a little more money, families can pay for a smuggler to book the bus tickets in advance, so migrants just show up and hop from one bus to the next."[53]

An Associated Press article included this description of the service provided by an "independent contractor" who facilitated travel through Mexico:

> He said he charges $2,500 for the trip from the Guatemalan border to the U.S. border, where he gives Central American migrants fake Mexican identity cards and makes them learn the first stanza of the Mexican national anthem before handing them off to another smuggler. Hopefully, if they are apprehended in the U.S., they'll only be sent back to Mexico, where they can try again.[54]

Other sources describe how migrants traveling on their own can choose to ride a freight train for part of their journey north (popularly known as La Bestia, or "the Beast") that may cost nothing, apart from payment to criminals in order to avoid harm.[55]

The Difficulty of Calculating Human-Smuggling Profits

Although profitability might say more about the financial health and viability of smuggling operations than revenue, profit estimation poses substantially greater challenges. The diversity of business models, and differentiation of smugglers' services among and within models, can yield substantial variation in smuggling fees and, possibly, in the smugglers' profits.[56] For these same reasons—as well as inherent data limitations (see Chapters 1 and 3) and the far greater scarcity of data on smugglers' costs—profit estimation is extremely difficult.[57] As noted elsewhere in this report, some scholars call into question whether it is even possible to undertake economic assessments in this arena, because of both illegality and data deficiencies.[58]

Nevertheless, we found scattered evidence on the reported costs to smugglers for discrete services they provide that, in combination with the evidence on fees cited previously and explored more thoroughly in Chapter 3, could say something about profitability. For example, some reporting describes smuggling organizations that recruit larger numbers of clients can pool

[53] Cleek, 2018.

[54] Associated Press, 2014.

[55] See, for example, the description of how migrants may be pushed off the trains if they don't pay protection fees, in Domingo Villegas (2014). For additional reporting on fees and costs, see Tiempo.hn (2017).

[56] As noted in Chapter 3, the smuggler's "accounting profits" might not equate to "economic profits."

[57] For additional comments on the paucity of data on smugglers' costs, see United Nations Office on Drugs and Crime, 2011, p. 85.

[58] Sanchez, 2017, 2018.

migrants and transport them great distances in tractor trailers or on charter buses, sometimes all the way across Mexico.[59]

A handful of press reports offers more detail on specific costs borne by smugglers. One set of data points on logistics costs, possibly originating in a 2014 Associated Press report, shows up intermittently across news sources and over time and recounts various transportation, lodging, and other costs incurred by smugglers that might sum to around $2,000 or more per migrant.[60] As presented in the 2014 Associated Press report:

- guide who makes the trip: $500–$600
- boatmen at Mexico's southern border: $1.50 to cross Suchiate River from Guatemala
- lodging: $11.50 a room, which can hold many migrants
- Central American gang: At least $100 per migrant to board Mexican freight train known as La Bestia, or "the Beast"
- Mexican police and immigration officials: $230–$540 to pass; $25–$40 per person to free detained migrant[61]
- drug cartels: $250–$300 for Mexican migrant, $500–$700 for Central American, about $1,500 for someone from Europe or Asia, plus 10 percent flat fee per smuggler to cross northern Mexico to the U.S. border
- boatmen at Mexico's northern border: $100 per immigrant to cross Rio Grande into the United States
- drivers: $150 for ride from Rio Grande to stash house; $200 for ride north of the U.S. Border Patrol's highway checkpoint to Houston
- caretaker at stash house: $20 per person per day.

An online magazine in Mexico that interviewed smugglers bringing unlawful migrants from El Salvador to the United States in 2017 identified three different coyotes involved in a loose network: one was based in El Salvador and coordinated the journey, one traveled with the unlawful migrants until the U.S.-Mexico border, and a third took the clients across the land border and to Houston. Before 2017, the fees charged to unlawful migrants totaled $8,000 to Houston, but after the increased enforcement by U.S. authorities in 2017, the coyotes were now asking for $9,500–$10,000. Of this total:

- $2,000 covered expenses to get to Reynosa (including corruption of police checkpoints in Guatemala and Mexico, transport, housing, food)
- $300 covered the "cartel fee," or *piso*

---

[59] Caldwell, 2018.

[60] These data have appeared in an online article authored by *Daily Mail* and Associated Press Reporters (2014), citing "Migrants, Coyotes, Court Testimony." This same material has also appeared in several other press reports, with some dated at about the same time as the *Daily Mail* article and some as recently as 2016 and 2017.

[61] It seems unlikely that the fee to free a detainee would be less than the fee to pass by, as implied.

- $5,000 paid for the coyote in charge of U.S. border crossing and the travel to Houston (an additional $1,500 was charged if the unlawful migrants wanted to travel past Houston into the interior)
- $1,000 went to the coyote who traveled through Mexico with the unlawful migrants
- $1,700 was the profit earned by the individual who facilitated the overall journey.[62]

A 2018 news article broke down the costs incurred by smugglers involved with the last leg of the journey for those seeking to evade detection while crossing into California. A smuggler specializing in bringing unlawful migrants from Mexicali to Los Angeles claimed to make up to $2,500 per unlawful migrant of the $5,000 to $6,500 that he charged. Of this fee,

> The biggest share, $2,800 to $3,000, goes to the guy driving the migrants to Los Angeles, because he's taking the biggest risk if caught by the Border Patrol. Alexis pays another $100 to $300 per migrant to polleros who work as decoys, lookouts, pickups, or who operate safe houses in Calexico. Alexis says he also has to pay off the Mexican police. They get $200 per migrant.[63]

Lastly, one smuggler interviewed by the Mexican newspaper *El Universal* noted that smugglers in general were making millions of dollars, but in their view most of these profits were being generated from crossings into the United States from Mexico.[64]

The evidence, albeit sparse, suggests that the actors that coordinate the overall travel of unlawful migrants may be netting up to $2,000 per journey, while the actors that coordinate illegal entries between POEs may be netting up to $2,500 per crossing. Others along the line, including the stash house operators who charge a few dollars a day to accommodate migrants, the lookouts who help coyotes avoid law enforcement, and those who transport migrants at various points in the journey, might see substantially less. However, because of the extremely limited data on potential profits that we were able to identify, we did not believe it was possible to generate a credible estimate for profits, and, as addressed in Chapter 3, it is unclear whether these figures would hold up more generally—or in relation to DHS or EMIF Sur data on fees—and how much "economic" profit would remain after accounting for risk.

Drug-Trafficking TCOs' Involvement in Human Smuggling

The most direct interaction between human smugglers and drug-trafficking organizations, many or most of which clearly manifest the attributes of TCOs, involves the payment of a one-time "tax," referred to at different parts of the border as a toll, mafia fee, or *piso,* that provides migrants with access to smuggling corridors on the U.S.-Mexico border under the control of drug traffickers. The open literature and interviews with SMEs suggest broad agreement about the

---

[62] Martinez, 2017.

[63] González and Solis, 2017.

[64] Castellano, 2014.

existence of this financial relationship;[65] however, they raise questions about the extent to which these markets and networks overlap more generally.

Human smugglers and drug traffickers conduct similar activities—providing illicit transportation services across international borders—and do so along common smuggling corridors, suggesting opportunities for overlapping business. Some sources suggest that drug-trafficking TCOs have greater financial incentive to participate in human-smuggling activities because smuggling fees have increased in recent years, but the data on trends in fees are mixed, as discussed in Chapter 3.[66] While the open literature is thin in this area, much of it suggests only minimal convergence between human smuggling and drug trafficking, beyond the collection of the *piso*, deconfliction of smuggling routes along the U.S.-Mexico border,[67] and, possibly, strategic use of human smuggling to draw attention from drug trafficking.[68] Several reports suggest that migrants, on occasion, carry drugs across the U.S.-Mexico border in exchange for reduced fees,[69] and other sources suggest that elements of certain drug-trafficking TCOs, particularly Los Zetas, have attempted to play a more direct role in human-smuggling activities.[70] However, our literature review and discussions with SMEs provided little evidence of a broader convergence of these networks and business operations.

Paying the Tax, or Piso

Over the past decade, the landscape of Mexico's main drug-trafficking TCOs has been characterized by a trend toward fragmentation and splintering, with the emergence of new groups that compete or collaborate with traditional groups.[71] However, despite the fluid nature of these organizations, a handful maintain control of most of the primary trafficking corridors into the

---

[65] For example,

> The most commonly reported interaction between migrants and drug traffickers—and perhaps the only one pointing to the existence of a structured system of financial transactions connecting drug trafficking and migrant facilitators—involved the payment of piso, a one-time toll to access specific parts of the migrant trail under the control of a [drug-trafficking organization]. (Sanchez and Zhang, 2018, p. 141)

[66] Weden, 2016; Olson, 2016; Slack and Whiteford, 2013.

[67] For example, "'Drug traffickers dictate where and when illegal crossings occur,' he said. 'Human smugglers arrange crossings through their 'business relationship' with drug traffickers'" (Prendergast, 2017).

[68] Cabrera, 2015; Slack and Campbell, 2016. The latter write that "Migrants in Altar were consistently being sent in staggered groups of 10 or 20 each half hour with a group of burreros behind the last group as a way to distract the border patrol" (p. 13).

[69] See, for example, Prendergast, 2017; Burnett, 2011.

[70] See, for example, Gallagher's (2018) description of Los Zetas coordinating the movement of tractor-trailers with up to 100 migrants inside.

[71] Beittel, 2018.

United States.[72] Such control allows these groups to both regulate and tax illicit trade through these territories, whether the trade occurs between or at POEs.[73] The purpose of regulating these movements is partly to ensure that other smuggling activities do not disrupt a drug-trafficking TCO's main drug-trafficking business, for example, by attracting the attention of authorities to key smuggling corridors. As such, drug traffickers would coordinate with human smugglers to deconflict and strategically position their activities and tell them when and where to move migrants across the U.S. border.

Controlling prime smuggling territory also affords drug-trafficking TCOs an opportunity to charge a tax on unlawful migrants seeking to pass through on their way to the United States. These protection payments or security fees function as tolls or taxes and are known to migrants as mafia fees, or *pisos*, depending on the region of the border.[74] According to U.S. government sources, it is all but impossible for migrants to cross some sections of the border, particularly those most tightly controlled by the drug traffickers, without paying the tax.[75]

Collecting the *piso* requires fairly extensive regulation of migrants passing through a drug-trafficking organization's territory, pointing to coordination between human smugglers and drug traffickers before a migrant reaches the U.S.-Mexico border. Migrants are often given a *clave* (or code) that indicates that they "belong to" or have been traveling with a particular human-smuggling organization, and they must provide this *clave* to lookouts who are affiliated with the drug-trafficking TCOs when they enter a border town.[76] Migrants traveling on their own are approached by lookouts and signed up by a smuggling group that requires payment of the *piso*. This system of regulation by drug-trafficking TCOs also depends on retribution against migrants or smugglers who do not pay the *piso* or follow directions about when and where to smuggle. Reports suggest the drug trafficker will kidnap, torture, and sometimes kill migrants and smugglers who do not do as instructed.[77]

Potential for Broader Convergence of Human Smuggling and Drug Trafficking

Whereas we found evidence in the open literature and SME interviews that suggests financial transactions and coordination among human smugglers and drug traffickers, we found little to

---

72 U.S. Department of Justice, Drug Enforcement Administration, 2017.

73 See, for example, the transcript of a *60 Minutes* episode (Pelley, 2018) in which drug-trafficking TCOs are described as a "regulatory mechanism" on the border that "essentially set the rules, so to speak, for illegal activities in the region. It has led to this professionalization, this need to collaborate and coordinate with the drug cartels." See also Leutert, 2017.

74 Kulish, 2018.

75 Olson, 2016; Nixon and Heisler, 2018.

76 Olson, 2016.

77 Slack and Campbell, 2016, pp. 12–18.

suggest broader convergence.[78] In particular, evidence that drug-trafficking TCOs are directly involved in human-smuggling operations is lacking. Although some sources suggest that drug traffickers may sometimes force migrants to carry backpacks of drugs across the border, it is not clear how common this practice is.[79] Studies that include testimonials of migrants suggest they are often motivated by financial considerations,[80] and it appears that drug-trafficking TCOs commonly waive the *piso* for migrants that carry drug loads, and sometimes pay them.[81] In this scenario, migrants who do not have enough money to pay for the final leg of their journey sometimes agree to carry drugs in lieu of payment.

We also uncovered reports suggesting that some drug-trafficking TCOs, specifically Los Zetas, are attempting to profit from human smuggling beyond the collection of a tax near the U.S.-Mexico border and have even established affiliates in some of Mexico's southern states and Central American countries.[82] If true, these activities appear to be more focused on extorting migrants than transportation them. For example, Los Zetas affiliates reportedly collected fees from migrants boarding freight trains in southern Mexico.[83] In addition, some of these reports of drug-trafficking TCOs' activities are inconsistent with other studies, including ones involving testimonials from migrant smugglers who operate on the U.S.-Mexico border, suggesting that drug-trafficking groups tend not to become directly involved in transporting migrants.[84] These studies suggest that human smuggling and drug trafficking are separate businesses and indicate that human smugglers are deterred from engaging in drug trafficking because of the risks of retribution and because it could harm their primary business, which depends on referrals.[85] A perception that human smugglers are members of drug-trafficking organizations that are known to extort and kidnap migrants might hurt business.

These studies similarly highlight the disincentives for drug traffickers to become more involved in human smuggling, principally because of the comparatively smaller profit margins involved in smuggling people as opposed to drugs. As one study notes: "In economic terms,

---

[78] Sanchez and Zhang, 2018, pp. 135–151.

[79] Leutert, 2017.

[80] See, for example, Sanchez and Zhang, 2018, p. 143:

> In our study, respondents' testimonies indicated that the decision to carry drugs often was a personal, complex choice, rather than the result of coercion. Lacking financial resources to cover basic needs like room or board, or having run out of money after traveling vast distances and no longer able to afford smuggling fees, some migrants opted to assist drug traffickers in exchange for financial compensation or transportation within the United States.

[81] Sanchez and Zhang, 2018.

[82] International Crisis Group, 2016.

[83] Farah and Lum, 2013.

[84] Palacios, 2014.

[85] Palacios, 2014.

taking control of migrant smuggling networks (does) not make sense: why engage in the complex activities this business requires when criminals can make large revenues from (smugglers) without doing anything themselves?"[86]

Conclusion

Our literature review and interviews with SMEs at DHS revealed that many different types of actors are involved in facilitating the movement of unlawful migrants from the NT of Central America to the United States. These smugglers reside on a spectrum that ranges from independent operators to more-formal networks. Only some of these networks appear to meet the statutory definition of a TCO, in that many do not appear to be "self-perpetuating," use violence and corruption systematically, or feature a truly transnational organizational structure. In line with this diversity of actors, smugglers also offer a wide array of services to unlawful migrants, spanning "pay-as-you-go" and "all-inclusive" arrangements. While the routes that unlawful migrants take are well established and primarily follow overland transportation networks, these migrants make use of various conveyances along the route depending on their needs and the fees they pay. Lastly, unlawful migrants generally are required to pay taxes, or *pisos*, to drug-trafficking TCOs along the U.S.-Mexico border for the right to pass through their territory, either directly or through human smugglers.

---

[86] Palacios, 2014.

3. Preliminary Findings on Revenue Estimation

Drawing from the principles of the general framework presented in Chapter 1, we set about estimating revenues from human smuggling, without regard to the type of smuggler. As discussed in Chapter 2, we found that we could not attribute smuggling revenues to particular types of smugglers, although we could evaluate the taxes, or *pisos*, that migrants pay drug-trafficking TCOs to traverse their territory. Unlike the revenue from smuggling fees, the entirety of the revenue from the tax goes to TCOs, specifically drug-trafficking TCOs, that control certain transit routes and border crossings.

Figure 3.1 depicts the flows of revenues associated with human smuggling to human smugglers of all types, including TCOs, and to drug-trafficking TCOs. The larger oval to the right represents the former, designated as "aggregate" smuggling revenue, and the smaller oval to the left represents the latter, designated as "tax" revenue. The intersection of the two ovals represents instances in which smuggling fees cover the tax.

Figure 3.1. Revenues to and Types of Actors Engaged in Human Smuggling

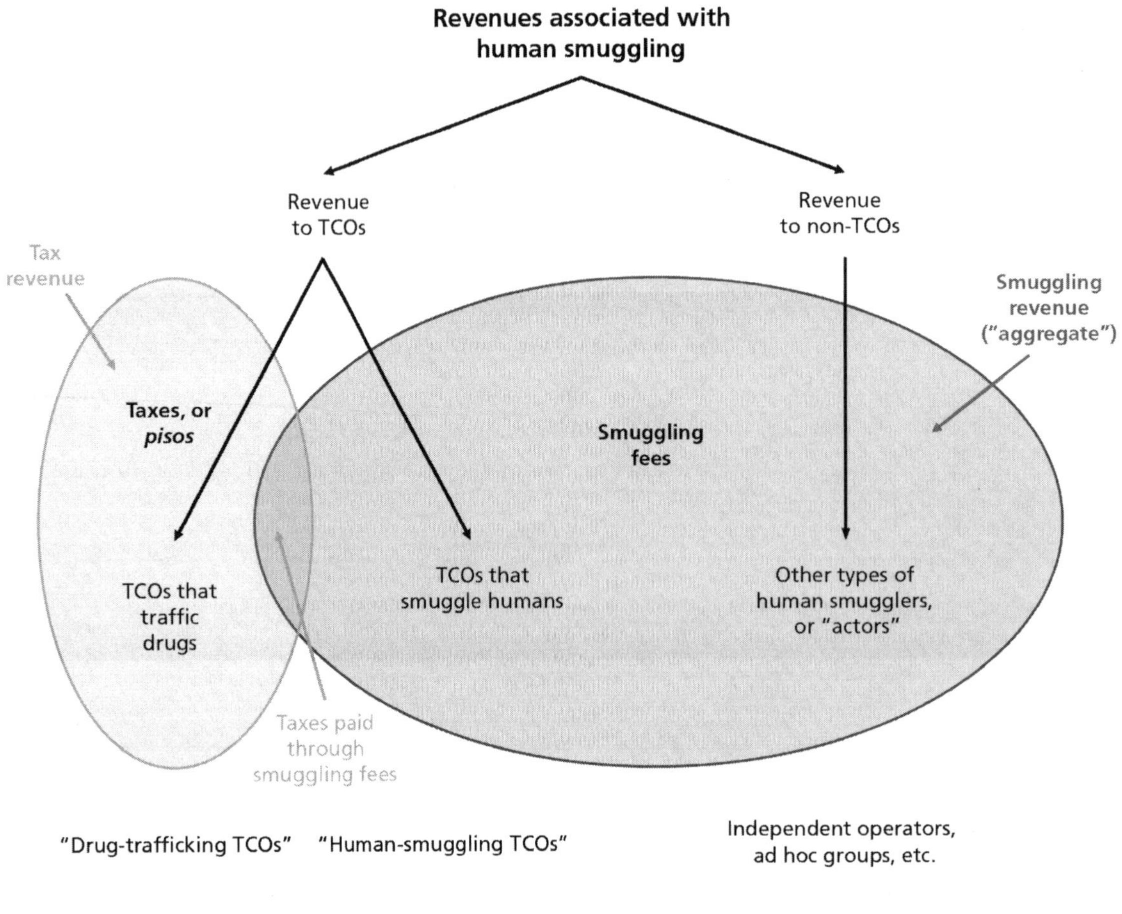

To estimate revenue to all types of human smugglers (i.e., aggregate smuggling revenue) along routes from the NT to the United States, we needed data on three variables: (1) the number of unlawful migrants along a route, (2) the percentage of those migrants who hire smugglers, and (3) the typical payments made, per migrant, to smugglers. Lacking data for specific routes from the NT to the United States, we defined three general routes, by country of origin, as "Guatemala–United States," "Honduras–United States," and "El Salvador–United States"; however, for our high-end estimate, we were also able to differentiate between payments en route to the U.S.-Mexico border as one "segment" of the journey and payments across that border as another segment.

Separately, we developed an ancillary, preliminary estimate for drug-trafficking TCOs' *piso* collections. If migrants hire a smuggler, they might pay the taxes through him or her, as a conduit; alternatively they might pay the taxes directly to the TCO, in which case the taxes would not be included in the smuggling fee. In either case, we could still attribute the payments directly to drug-trafficking TCOs.

For each variable, we present ranges of estimates, based on various assumptions about behavior and markets and data from DHS and other sources, as discussed below. We analyzed data from 2015–2017 or earlier, but, unless noted otherwise, we worked with the most recent available data (2017) for each step of the analysis.[87]

Flows of Unlawful Migrants

We developed a range of estimates for unlawful migrant flows from DHS data on "apprehensions," "got-aways," and "turn-backs" between POEs at the southwest border and from estimates of apprehension rates, also between POEs.[88] By implication, the data omit activity at POEs, including arrivals of unaccompanied children and families that present themselves to border officials, without attempting evasion, which we address separately, below.

In this context, an *apprehension* is an unlawful migrant who U.S. Border Patrol agents apprehend at the U.S. border; a *got-away* is "a subject who, after making an illegal entry, is not turned back or apprehended"; and a *turn-back* is "a subject who, after making an illegal entry into the United States, returns to the country from which he or she entered, not resulting in an apprehension or got away."[89] Reported apprehensions, got-aways, and turn-backs are parts of the

---

[87] In some instances, such as those of unlawful migrant flows, we looked at data as far back as 2012, but given a spike in reported apprehensions and, hence, in apparent flows in 2014 (see Figure 3.2), we chose to work primarily with the data after that year.

[88] DHS provided us with the underlying data for apprehensions, got-aways, and turn-backs and the point estimates for the so-called "partial apprehension rate" that is depicted in DHS Office of Immigration Statistics, 2017, p. 8, Figure 3. (The estimates in that study extend only as far as 2016, so we applied the 2016 rate to the 2017 data.) We then used these data and the point estimates for the apprehension rate to construct its estimates on flows.

[89] DHS Office of Immigration Statistics, 2017, p. 5.

"known flows," either by direct observation or by inference, e.g., because of camera views, sensor activations, or other evidence. As discussed in Appendix C, researchers have developed methods to estimate the apprehension rate, which is the share of apprehensions in total attempted border crossings, and overcome the analytical obstacle of unobserved and uninferred got-aways (i.e., "unknown flows").[90] An estimate of migrant flows that makes use of this rate should be more complete than an estimate that makes use of the data on reported got-aways, but the methods for estimating apprehension rate are also imperfect.[91]

We undertook four sets of calculations of unlawful migrant flows (see Appendix C), using two basic methods—one with data on reported got-aways and one with estimates of the apprehension rate—and different combinations of the data on turn-backs, to account for uncertainty about the behavior of turn-backs.[92] First, at the low end, we calculated total flows from each NT country to the United States as the sum of just the apprehensions and got-aways from that country, assuming that all turn-backs will try to cross into the United States again and, eventually, will be apprehended or get away.[93] Second, we dropped that assumption and treated turn-backs as an additive category, with total flows consisting of the sum of apprehensions, got-aways, and turn-backs. Third, we divided apprehensions by the apprehension rate to account for unknown flows, without regard to turn-backs. Fourth, at the high end, we applied the same apprehension rate, but added turn-backs. Got-aways are not included in the final calculation because they are assumed to have been included in the operation involving the apprehension rate.

We found that the range progressed steadily from the low to the high end, but the difference in methods—the use of got-aways or the apprehension rate—accounted for substantially more of the bump-up than the inclusion of turn-backs in either approach.

On that basis, migrant flows from the NT in 2017 could have been as low as about 218,000 and as high as about 345,000, with Guatemala accounting for the largest share, just over 88,000, or about 40 percent, of either estimate (see Figure 3.2).[94] However, the low-end figure is almost certainly too low, because U.S. Border Patrol agents cannot observe or infer every got-away.[95]

---

[90] Estimation is necessary because of the "denominator problem" (see, e.g., DHS Office of Immigration Statistics, 2017, p. 3). To obtain an apprehension rate, one must divide the number of apprehensions by the total number of attempted border crossings, both failed and successful, which include got-aways that cannot be observed or inferred fully. See also Morral, Willis, and Brownell, 2011.

[91] For an overview of various limitations that might make the rate too high or too low, see DHS Office of Immigration Statistics, 2017, pp. 7–8.

[92] With some adaptation to account for uncertainty about the behavior of turn-backs and the limitations of each approach, we drew from concepts and methods presented in DHS Office of Immigration Statistics, 2017.

[93] Lacking country-specific data on turn-backs and got-aways, we assumed that a country's share of all turn-backs and got-aways at the border was the same as its share of all apprehensions at the border. U.S. Border Patrol agents observe turn-backs and got-aways without knowledge of their origin.

[94] These estimates do not include migrants who are apprehended in Mexico or elsewhere en route and do not, eventually, make their way to the U.S.-Mexico border as either an apprehension, turn-back, or got-away. Rodríguez

Figure 3.2. Estimated Flows of Migrants from the Northern Triangle to the United States

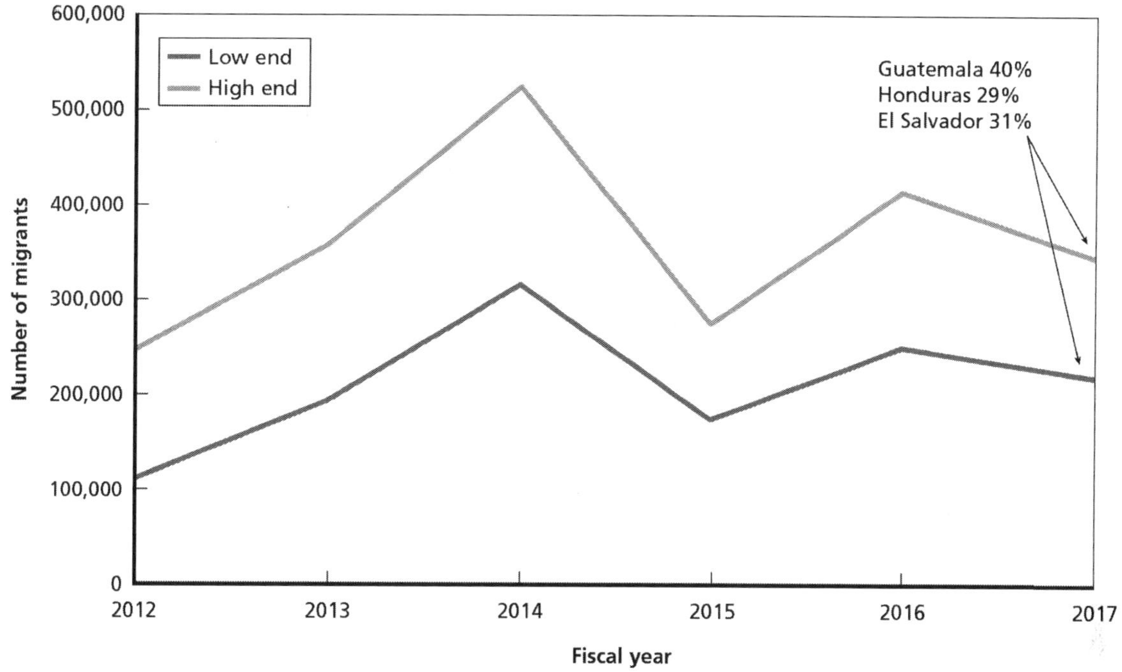

SOURCE: Author calculations, based on fiscal-year data provided by DHS.

Given modest rates of recidivism for Central Americans in the DHS data, e.g., less than 5 percent for migrants from each NT country in 2017,[96] we did not adjust the flow data for individuals who try to enter the United States repeatedly. However, failure to make an adjustment will result in an upward bias in the preliminary estimates of smuggling revenue, by "double counting" some fees, if migrants purchase a package of smuggling services that includes multiple journeys and need a second or third try (see Chapter 2).

We include a short discussion of the implications of omitting both activity at POEs, which might bias the revenue estimate downward, and adjustments for recidivism, which might bias it upward, after presenting the preliminary revenue estimate.

Chávez (2016, p. 9) provides a broader, preliminary estimate of flows of Central American migrants in 2015 that is higher than the DHS-derived, high-end estimate for that year: i.e., 377,000 as compared with 291,000.

[95] Recent research in this arena (e.g., Egan et al., 2018; DHS Office of Immigration Statistics, 2017) has focused on establishing interdiction effectiveness, apprehension rates, and, by extension, successful entries or got-aways. As a related matter, Hale et al. (2018) present estimates of smuggling capacity along routes from Guatemala to the United State that are roughly consistent with our medium-to-high-end estimates for Guatemala.

[96] We calculated recidivism rates as shares of unique NT migrants, based on fingerprint identification numbers, who try to enter the United States and are apprehended more than once in a given period, e.g., a year.

Percentage of Unlawful Migrants Hiring Smugglers

For insight into the percentage of unlawful migrants who hire smugglers to help them get from the NT to the United States, we drew data from both DHS and EMIF Sur, a survey conducted at the Mexico-Guatemala border by the Colegio de la Frontera Norte, which is located in Mexico.[97]

As discussed in other research, the DHS data on migrants' use of smugglers might fail to capture a substantial amount of smuggling activity.[98] One group of researchers noted in 2010 that the "primary concern is that the reported use of smugglers by apprehended migrants in the administrative record is much lower than the reported use of smugglers in migrant survey data," including the EMIF Sur data.[99] It is also lower than one might expect from anecdotal evidence (see Chapter 2) and from our conversations with SMEs. By our calculation, about 32, 22, and 14 percent of the NT migrants in the DHS data reported use of smugglers in 2015, 2016, and 2017, respectively, whereas a 2018 publication from the EMIF Sur data suggests upward of 60 to 65 percent over that period,[100] consistently, and SMEs tend to agree that many or most NT migrants hire a smuggler at some point.[101]

A 2017 publication from the EMIF Sur data offers country-specific figures and suggests slightly lower use rates, ranging from 46.6 percent for migrants from Honduras in 2015 to 66.2 percent for migrants from Guatemala in 2016.[102] For 2017, that source reports 63.4, 61.1, and 57.5 percent for migrants from Guatemala, Honduras, and El Salvador, respectively.

On the basis of those sources, about 25 to 67 percent of NT migrants might have hired smugglers in recent years, with some variation by country of origin. Given difficulty reconciling the country-specific and regional data within and across sources, we chose to work with that broad range, regardless of the route or year under consideration.[103]

---

97 The EMIF website sets out objectives of the survey at the southern border, e.g., to "increase understanding of the flows of migrants who cross between Mexico and Guatemala in order to work in Mexico or the United States, along with the undocumented migrants that cross Mexican territory and are returned to Guatemala, Honduras and El Salvador by Mexican and U.S. immigration officials" (EMIF, undated-b). For this report, we focused on undocumented migrants from the three NT countries who are returned by U.S. immigration officials, not those returned by Mexican officials. For information about the survey methodology, see EMIF, undated-c.

98 Roberts et al., 2010; Sanchez, 2016.

99 Roberts et al., 2010, p. 2.

100 EMIF Sur, 2018b, p. 3, Chart 8.

101 Similarly, Hale et al. (2018) asked 270 Central American migrants, "Did someone help or facilitate you make your journey?" and 69 percent of respondents said "yes."

102 EMIF Sur, 2018a, p. 5, Chart 9b.

103 Given more time, we would have appealed to the underlying EMIF Sur data, which are available online, to reconcile the country-specific and regional figures and refine the estimate. As for a trend, the DHS data show a pronounced decline in migrants' use of smugglers over the past three years, but the EMIF Sur data do not.

Separate from those estimates, we postulated, based on conversations with SMEs and information found in the literature, that about half or more migrants, say 50 to 75 percent, pay some form of tax, or *piso*, to drug-trafficking TCOs that they "encounter" on their journeys, regardless of whether they are working with a smuggler or traveling on their own. SMEs indicated that nearly all migrants pay the tax along some routes. Consistent with the proposed range, a taxation rate of about 60 percent of migrants appears in a recent study of organized crime and Central American migration in Mexico.[104]

Human-Smuggling Fees and Payments

For this calculation, we also drew from DHS and EMIF Sur data and turned to other sources, including our interviews with SMEs.

To start, we used the DHS data to calculate mean and median smuggling fees as reported to U.S. Border Patrol agents by unlawful migrants who are apprehended at the U.S.-Mexico border, between POEs. It is our understanding that the reported fees should cover those migrants' payments to smugglers along the entire route, from the NT into the United States, including fees for travel within the United States, but that the figures might not include all payments. For example, they might only encompass fees for part of the journey, e.g., to the U.S. border, or *pisos* paid to drug-trafficking TCOs.

In data plots, we observed a large number of low-end fees, which might validate concerns about fragmentation or simply reflect the migrants' preferences for inexpensive, pay-as-you-go services (see Chapter 2). We also found extreme high-end outliers, possibly indicating confusion over currency or data entry errors.

In 2017, the averages of the reported smuggling fees in the DHS data were about $4,700 per person for Guatemalan migrants, $3,800 per person for Honduran migrants, $4,600 per person for Salvadorian migrants, and about $4,400 per person for NT migrants overall.[105] (See Appendix D, Table D.1, for more information about the properties of the DHS data.) The median figures for the same year were similar but predictably lower, given the density of low-end observations, the presence of high-end outliers, and considerable other "noise" in the data, with $4,000 for Guatemalan migrants, $3,000 for Honduran migrants, $4,000 for Salvadorian migrants, and $4,000 for NT migrants overall. These mean and median figures were less than expected, given recent press reports (discussed in Chapter 2) and conversations with some SMEs that suggested fees ranging from $6,000 to $10,000 or more but, as noted above, could also reflect migrants' preferences for particular or fewer services.

---

[104] Leutert, 2018.

[105] We also calculated an adjusted mean for each country, by removing observations greater or less than two standard deviations from the unadjusted mean, but this approach had no effect at the low end because there were no observations below the two-standard-deviation threshold.

For comparative purposes, we also looked at the EMIF Sur data on migrants' actual and agreed payments to smugglers. EMIF Sur asks Guatemalan, Honduran, and Salvadorian migrants who have been returned to their respective countries of origin by U.S. immigration officials how much they paid or agreed to pay to travel (1) from their home country, through Mexico, and to the U.S.-Mexico border and (2) from the U.S.-Mexico border into the United States.[106] The results from the EMIF Sur data, which might include some unrealized payments and more transit in the United States, were higher than the results from the DHS data and better aligned with expectations. The averages and medians for 2017 were similar, with averages of about $10,700, $10,600, and $8,000 for migrants from Guatemala, Honduras, and El Salvador, respectively, and with medians of about $10,300, $11,500, and $8,000 for migrants from Guatemala, Honduras, and El Salvador, respectively (see Appendix D, Table D.2).[107]

Figures 3.3a–3.3c compare mean and median smuggling fees across sources, by country of origin for 2015–2017. Whereas the EMIF Sur data indicate a possible upward trend in smuggling fees over the past three years, the DHS data do not.

Figure 3.3a. Guatemala: Mean and Median Values of Northern Triangle Migrants' Payments to Smugglers for 2015–2017, by Country of Origin and Data Source (in U.S. dollars)

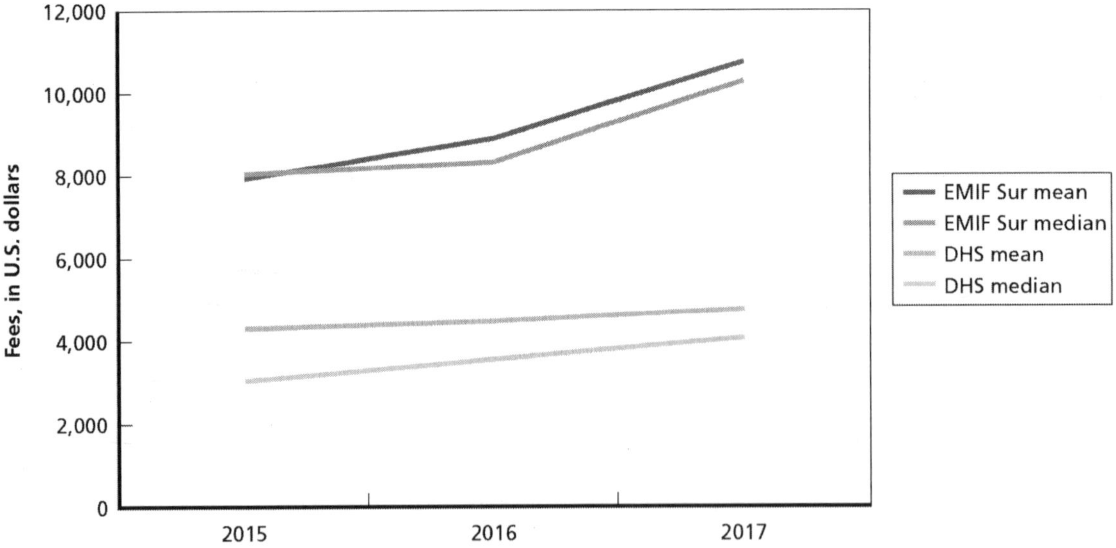

SOURCES: Author estimates based on EMIF Sur calendar-year data (EMIF, undated-a) and fiscal-year data provided by DHS.
NOTE: Cost estimates are in nominal U.S. dollars, using midyear exchange rates to adjust EMIF Sur data denominated in non-U.S. currencies (e.g., pesos or quetzals).

---

[106] EMIF Sur also asks similar questions of migrants who have been returned by Mexican immigration officials, but we did not work with those data.

[107] These figures are the sums of the means or medians, respectively, for each country for each segment, first, from the country of origin to the U.S. border and, second, across the U.S. border.

Figure 3.3b. Honduras: Mean and Median Values of Northern Triangle Migrants' Payments to Smugglers for 2015–2017, by Country of Origin and Data Source (in U.S. dollars)

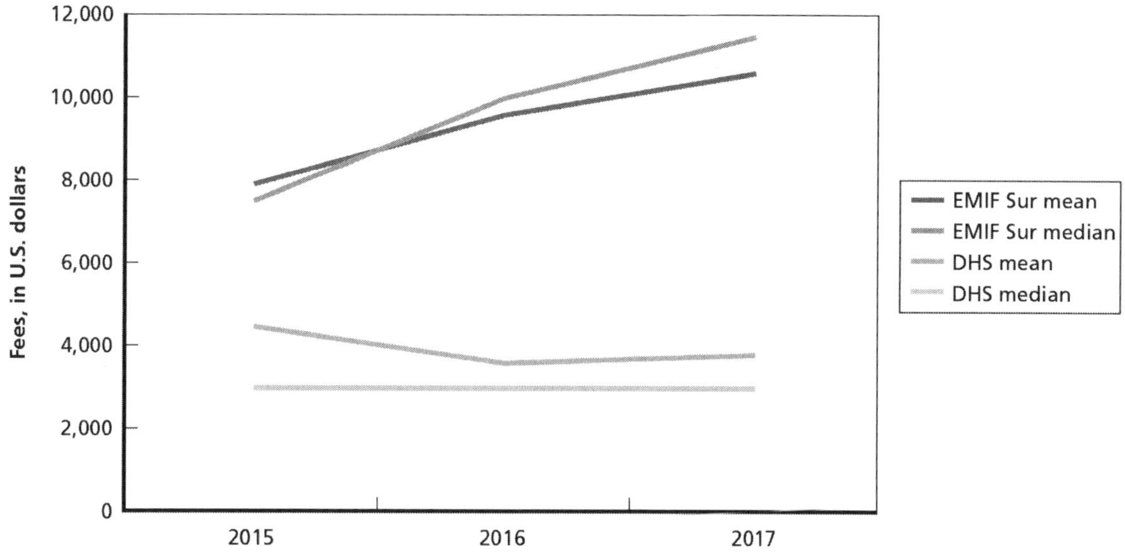

SOURCES: Author estimates based on EMIF Sur calendar-year data (EMIF, undated-a) and fiscal-year data provided by DHS.
NOTE: Cost estimates are in nominal U.S. dollars, using midyear exchange rates to adjust EMIF Sur data denominated in non-U.S. currencies (e.g., pesos or quetzals).

Figure 3.3c. El Salvador: Mean and Median Values of Northern Triangle Migrants' Payments to Smugglers for 2015–2017, by Country of Origin and Data Source (in U.S. dollars)

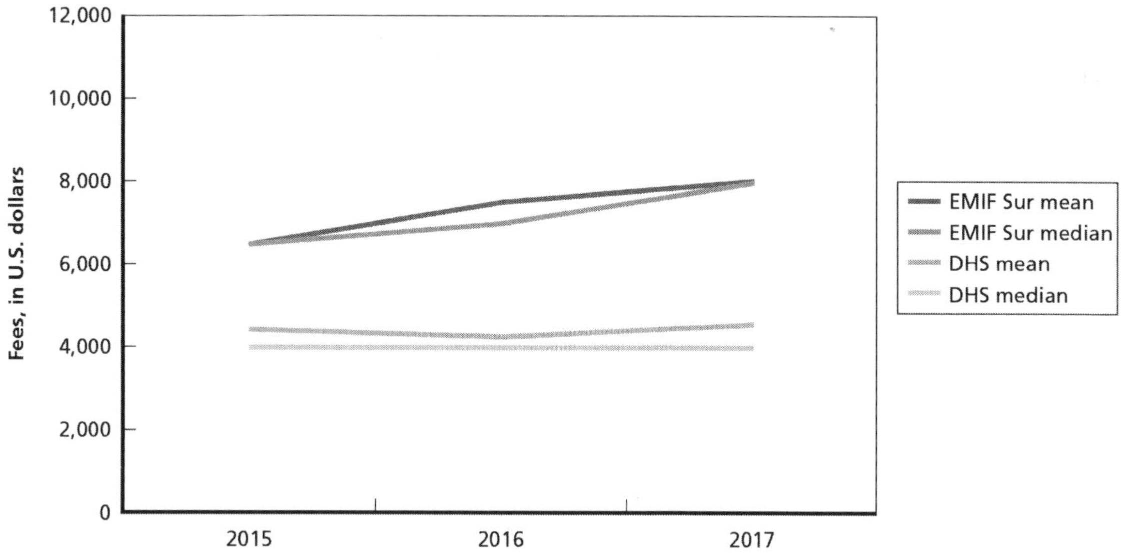

SOURCES: Author estimates based on EMIF Sur calendar-year data (EMIF, undated-a) and fiscal-year data provided by DHS.
NOTE: Cost estimates are in nominal U.S. dollars, using midyear exchange rates to adjust EMIF Sur data denominated in non-U.S. currencies (e.g., pesos or quetzals).

Taking the properties of the DHS and EMIF Sur data into account, we chose to work with the median values for the fees for each route in 2017 to create ranges. Route by route, the median value from the DHS data represents the low end, and the median value from the EMIF Sur data represents the high end (see Figure 3.4); for example, for the Honduras–United States route, the median values span $3,000 (from the DHS data) and $11,500 (from the EMIF Sur data).

Figure 3.4. Median Values of Northern Triangle Migrants' Payments to Smugglers in 2017, by Country of Origin and Data Source (in U.S. dollars)

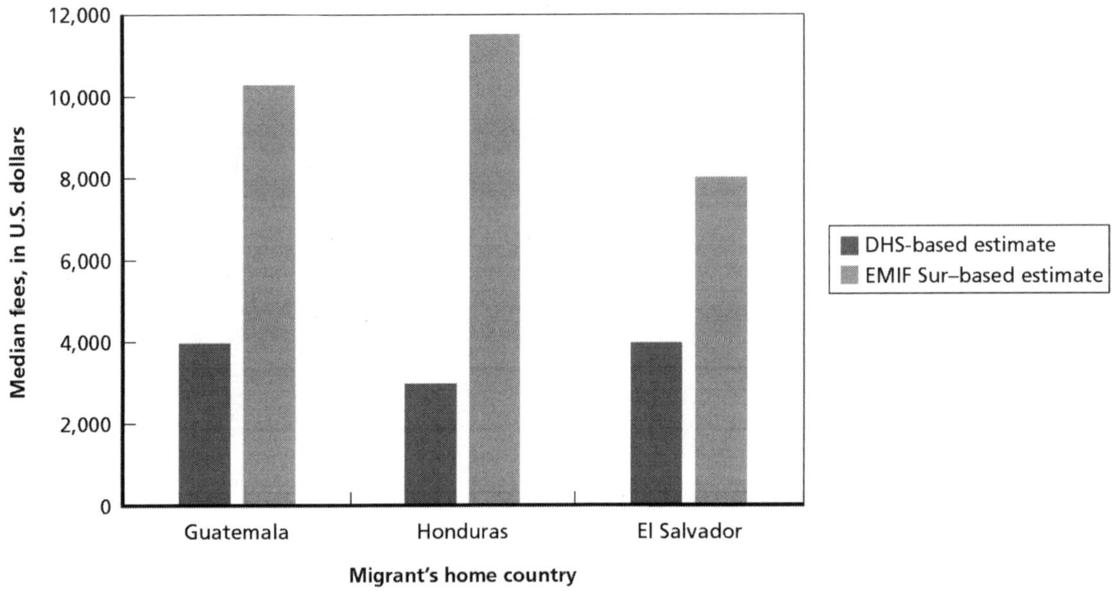

SOURCES: Author estimates based on EMIF Sur calendar-year data (EMIF, undated-a) and fiscal-year data provided by DHS.
NOTE: Cost estimates are in nominal U.S. dollars, using midyear exchange rates to adjust EMIF Sur data denominated in non-U.S. currencies (e.g., pesos or quetzals).

In addition, we found estimates of taxes, or *pisos*, paid to drug-trafficking TCOs' of about $300 per person on the low end[108] and about $500–$700 per person on the high end[109] in various press reports and in discussion with SMEs. For computational purposes, we used a range of $300 to $700 for migrants from all countries and without regard to year.

---

[108] See for example, a human smuggler's description of the $300 *cuota de cartel*, or cartel tax, that he has to pay in Martinez, 2017.

[109] These data have appeared in *Daily Mail* and Associated Press Reporters (2014) and elsewhere. One SME suggested a higher figure, i.e., about $1,100 for one transit zone, but this looked like an outlier.

Ranges of Estimates of Smuggling Revenues and *Piso* Collections

Working with ranges for each variable, we constructed a set of preliminary low- and high-end estimates of revenues to all types of smugglers in 2017, by route (Guatemala–United States, Honduras–United States, and El Salvador–United States) and for the NT overall. We did not attempt to parse those revenues by human-smuggling TCO, ad hoc group, independent operator, or other type of smuggler. We also developed an ancillary set of preliminary estimates for drug-trafficking TCOs' *piso* collections that might or might not add to the estimates of smuggling revenue.

Smuggling Revenues

For each general route from the NT to the United States, we constructed a preliminary estimate—or range of estimates—for smugglers' revenue from the low-end and high-end figures for (1) unlawful migrant flows, (2) the percentage of those migrants who use smugglers, and (3) the migrants' payments to smugglers. First, we multiplied the low-end figures for each route, and then we multiplied the high-end figures for each route, producing a corresponding low- and high-end estimate for each route. To illustrate a low-end calculation, using the 2017 data, for Guatemala, we multiplied the low-end flow estimate of just over 88,000 by the low-end use estimate of about 25 percent and then multiplied the product by the low-end fee estimate of about $4,000. The calculation resulted in a low-end, preliminary revenue estimate of $88 million dollars for the Guatemala–United States route in 2017.

To develop the corresponding high-end estimates, by route, we repeated the process, using the high-end estimates for each of the three variables on migrant flows, migrants' use of smugglers, and smuggling fees. At the high end, we also differentiated between payments en route to the U.S.-Mexico border, as one "segment" of the journey, and payments across the border, as another segment. We were able to draw this distinction because the EMIF Sur data on fees, which uniformly constitute the high end of the range, draw this distinction.

On that basis, smugglers' revenues from smuggling migrants from the three NT countries combined (as would correspond to the larger oval to the right in Figure 3.1) could have ranged from about $200 million to $2.3 billion, reflecting the considerable uncertainty of the underlying estimates of migrant flows, migrants' use of smugglers, and smuggling fees (see Table 3.1). At the high end, somewhat more revenue might accrue en route to the U.S.-Mexico border than across that border, and some of the revenue that accrues "across" might pertain to expenditures for domestic U.S. travel.

Table 3.1. Preliminary Estimates of Smuggling Revenues, by Country of Origin for 2017 (In millions of U.S. dollars)

	Total into United States		To U.S.-Mexico Border	Across U.S.-Mexico Border
Country of Origin	**Low End**	**High End**	**High End**	**High End**
Guatemala	88	957	574	383
Honduras	48	768	434	334
El Salvador	67	563	281	281
Total Northern Triangle	**203**	**2,288**	**1,290**	**998**

SOURCE: Author estimates based on analysis of DHS, EMIF Sur, and other data.

We have no basis for attributing the preliminary "aggregate" estimate of smuggling revenue to any particular type of smuggler, be it TCO or not, but the preponderance of the evidence (see Chapter 2) suggests that much of the revenue from smuggling would not accrue to organizations that one might identify as TCOs, based on official definitions.

At the outset and at each stage of the calculations, we encountered analytical challenges that might suggest, in some instances, that the low end of the preliminary revenue estimate is too low, and, in other instances, that the high end is too high. For example, at the low end, the data are missing observations on got-aways, and, at the high end, the data might include some agreed payments that never materialize.[110] But, some analytical challenges could have affected both ends of the range. In particular, we worked with data on apprehensions between POEs, which meant excluding potentially relevant activity at POEs and undercounting migrant flows, and we did not make any adjustments for recidivism, which introduced the possibility of double counting fees and overstating revenue.

To better understand the implications of omitting POE activity and recidivism adjustments, we undertook two sets of side calculations to account, first, for the missing activity and, second, for possible double counting. In the first instance, if one were to assume that unaccompanied children and families that present themselves to authorities at POEs use smuggling services to travel to the U.S.-Mexico border in the same ways as other unlawful migrants, then, with that activity, the preliminary revenue estimate for all three routes, combined, could have been about 5.5 percent higher at the low end of the range and 3.3 percent higher at the high end.[111] In the second instance, if one were to reduce the preliminary estimates for each country of origin by the

[110] Recalling that the fee data from EMIF Sur include not just actual payments, but also agreed payments, the high end of the range might overstate actual revenues, whether before or after crossing the border.

[111] At the high end, we multiplied the number of unaccompanied children and family members who presented themselves at POEs in 2017, by country of origin, by the high-end percentage of use and the EMIF Sur figures for smuggling fees, limited to transit as far as the U.S.-Mexico border, which amounted to 50–60 percent of the total, by country. At the low end, we multiplied the same flows by the low-end percentage and apportioned the DHS figures for fees, using the 50–60 percent shares found in the EMIF Sur data.

applicable recidivism rate, the estimate for the three routes, combined, would have been about 3.4 percent lower at both ends of the range.[112]

Drug-Trafficking TCOs' Piso *Collections*

Unlike the preliminary estimate of revenues from smuggling, the preliminary tax, or *piso*, estimate tracks directly to TCOs, specifically drug-trafficking TCOs. As previously, we arrived at a total value by multiplying migrant flows, by percentages, by payments, but, in this case, the percentages indicate "encounters" with the drug-trafficking TCOs rather than "use" of smugglers and the payments refer to taxes rather than fees. Whereas the migrant flow numbers were the same as for the foregoing revenue estimate, the relevant low- and high-end percentages for these calculations were 50 percent and 75 percent, the relevant payment figures were $300 and $700, and neither the percentages nor payments differed by route.[113]

On that basis, the total amount of *pisos* that unlawful migrants from the NT might have paid to drug-trafficking TCOs in 2017—for traveling the three routes, combined (as would correspond to the smaller oval to the left in Figure 3.1)—could have ranged from about $30 million to $180 million (see Table 3.2). Whether these sums would constitute a share of the foregoing revenue figures or an additional payment would depend, in part, on the smuggling arrangement and whether it was "all-inclusive." If the arrangement were all-inclusive, the tax might be folded into the smuggling fee (as depicted in the intersection of the two ovals in Figure 3.1), but it would, nevertheless, pass through to the drug-trafficking TCO that demanded payment for the migrant's passage.

Table 3.2. Preliminary Estimates of Drug-Trafficking TCOs' Tax, or *Piso*, Collections, by Country of Origin for 2017 (in millions of U.S. dollars)

Country of Origin	Low End	High End
Guatemala	13	73
Honduras	10	53
El Salvador	10	55
Total Northern Triangle	**33**	**181**

SOURCE: Author estimates based on analysis of DHS and other data.

[112] At the low and high end, we simply applied the recidivism rates, by country of origin, ranging from 2.5 to 4.5 percent, to the preliminary estimates of smuggling revenue, by country of origin.

[113] We recognized that TCOs have more or less control along certain routes and at certain border crossings, but we lacked the data to include that level of refinement in its tax estimates.

Profitability, Risk, and Other Economic Considerations

Our quantitative analysis has so far focused strictly on revenues, but profitability might be more relevant as a measure of human smuggling's contributions to the financial health and viability of TCOs and other smuggling operations. Unfortunately, the data on smugglers' costs, which would be necessary to calculate profit, are even scarcer than the data on revenue; we are unaware of any systematic collection of data on costs (see Chapter 2).[114]

We found scattered anecdotal evidence suggesting that smugglers' costs are nontrivial but that they could leave room for profit (see Chapter 2). For example, the press has reported transit costs that might sum to around $2,000 or more, depending on incidentals.[115] With costs at that level or even higher, smuggling could be "profitable," at least as an accounting matter, but perhaps not as an economic matter. Some of the difference between revenues and costs might constitute a "risk premium," or compensation for the risks that actors take on when they engage in human smuggling, such as those of a driver who transports unlawful migrants from the U.S.-Mexico border to Los Angeles. Given low barriers to entry in this market—that is, nearly anyone willing to bear the risks of smuggling can offer smuggling services—it is possible that competition among smugglers for migrants' business might drive economic profits to zero or near to zero, after compensating for the risk.

Other researchers admit the difficulty of profit estimation but also call profitability of almost any type into question.[116] One researcher asserts, "it is virtually impossible to estimate the size of the smuggling market. It is even harder to determine its profits, given its underground, unregulated nature."[117] But this researcher also suggests that profits tend to be modest and are absorbed locally. In a prior article, the same researcher finds that "individual facilitators earnings vary considerably," after accounting for all costs, and that "smuggling constitutes in the majority of cases only a supplemental income-generating strategy."[118]

The taxes, or *pisos*, that migrants pay to drug-trafficking TCOs present fewer analytical challenges insomuch as they might amount to pure or nearly pure profit. The TCOs that control particular transit routes and border crossings collect the tax, but they provide few reciprocal services (see Chapter 2). Even if a drug-trafficking TCO describes the payment as "protection" or "security," the protection is largely from the TCO itself. As for risk premium, it is possible that drug-trafficking TCOs incur some risk when they allow migrants to pass through their territory, but these TCOs might use the migrants' passage strategically to divert attention from or

---

[114] For additional comments on the paucity of data on smugglers' costs, see also United Nations Office on Drugs and Crime, 2011, p. 85.

[115] These figures appeared in *Daily Mail* and Associated Press Reporters (2014) and elsewhere.

[116] Sanchez, 2017, 2018.

[117] Sanchez, 2018, p. 2.

[118] Sanchez, 2017, p. 17.

conceal other illegal activities, such as drug smuggling, and to mitigate their risks.[119] In addition, drug-trafficking TCOs might also employ migrants as unremunerated "mules," or drug couriers, if the migrants cannot afford the *piso*.

---

[119] See, for example, Cabrera, 2015.

4. Concluding Remarks

In this scoping study, we set out to characterize TCOs that smuggle unlawful migrants from the NT of Central America (Guatemala, Honduras, and El Salvador) to the United States and to develop a preliminary estimate of the TCOs' smuggling revenues.

However, as the research progressed, it became clear that many different types of actors engage in human smuggling along those routes, only some of which appear to meet official definitions (in legislation and formal policy guidance) of a TCO. The literature presented strong evidence, confirmed by SMEs, that smugglers operating along the routes from the NT to the United States reside along a spectrum that ranges widely from independent operators, to ad hoc groups, to loose networks, to more-formal networks. Importantly, we could not identify the percentage of unlawful migrants that use each type of smuggler, and thus we could not distinguish the revenues that flow to human-smuggling TCOs from the revenues that flow to other actors engaged in human smuggling. However, we could separately identify the taxes, or *pisos*, that migrants pay to drug-trafficking TCOs to transit through their territory.

With those limitations in mind, we undertook a broader assessment of human smuggling, smugglers, and aggregate smuggling revenues. We developed preliminary estimates—ranges of estimates—of revenue from smuggling unlawful migrants along three routes, from Guatemala, Honduras, and El Salvador to the United States, without regard to the type of smuggler, be it a TCO, independent operator, or other type. We based the estimates on three variables: the flow of unlawful migrants from each country to the United States, the percentage of those migrants that use smugglers along the way, and the fees that the migrants pay to smugglers, each of which entailed estimation of its own.

On that basis, we developed a preliminary estimate of aggregate smuggling revenue—for the three routes, combined, in 2017—that ranged from about $200 million to $2.3 billion. This estimate is, as the range implies, highly uncertain, owing largely to a scarcity of reliable data for each variable. Likewise, we produced an ancillary and still preliminary estimate of drug-trafficking TCOs' *piso* collections that also spanned an order of magnitude, from about $30 million to $180 million.

The rest of this chapter focuses on implications of these findings for DHS for targeting human smuggling, informing resource allocation decisions, and improving data collection.

Targeting Human Smuggling

A key finding of this report is that human smuggling involves many different types of smugglers, or "actors," with organizations that are often informal and based on relationships instead of well-established hierarchies. Absent formality and strict hierarchical structures, it might be difficult for DHS to effectively target them with legal sanctions, for several reasons:

- Loose networks are difficult to disrupt, ad hoc groups are even less susceptible, and independent operators are easily replaceable. As described in Chapter 2, key actors associated with loose networks and involved in smuggling people north may not know each other well or at all, ad hoc groups are even less cohesive and more amenable to reconfiguration, and the independent operators that form part of both kinds of networks have immediate substitutes. This means that even if DHS can apply sanctions to some individuals in a given network or group or to individuals who operate independently, its ability to disrupt their organizations or affect the market may be limited.
- Low barriers to entry can further impede disruption. While individuals might face some personal risk when they engage in smuggling, they appear to engage fluidly—part-time or as opportunities present themselves—at least at low levels (e.g., taxi drivers and hotel or stash house operators) and possibly as facilitators. To build on the above example, this means that even if DHS can apply sanctions to such actors, the actors can generally be replaced easily, and others can fill their roles.
- Going after facilitators might be more fruitful, but doing so effectively might be challenging. To the extent that human-smuggling networks are hierarchical, their leaders are based in foreign countries (i.e., facilitators based in Mexico and the NT for the flows this report has addressed). This means that DHS must be able to work with partner agencies in those countries to apply sanctions to the leaders of these networks, which can be challenging. DHS can and does target individuals involved in human smuggling that are based in the United States, but, as discussed in Chapter 2, these actors are generally not prominent figures in human-smuggling networks, but rather subcontractors.

One area where DHS may be able to affect networks, groups, or the market involves money transfers that take place once individuals arrive in the United States. As noted in Chapter 2, many migrants only make their final payment to smugglers after they arrive in the United States. DHS might consider expanding existing efforts to investigate these kinds of payments, including working more closely with formal and informal banking services, to identify suspicious payments. DHS could also consider expanding current efforts to work with foreign law enforcement partners. As noted above, to the extent that human-smuggling networks are hierarchical, their leadership is almost always foreign-based. This means that DHS must work with foreign partners to effectively sanction the individuals involved.

Allocating Resources

Comparing the preliminary estimate of revenues from human smuggling to information about other types of illicit—and even licit—activities could help inform DHS's resource allocation decisions. For example, DHS might consider how much it should prioritize efforts to disrupt human-smuggling operations in light of other concerns about TCOs.

To approach that question, we searched for analogous estimates of TCOs' revenues from transporting illicit drugs through Mexico and across the U.S.-Mexico border and compared them to our preliminary estimate of revenues from human smuggling. Although we were not able to find recent estimates of drug-trafficking revenues, estimates developed in a 2010 RAND report for marijuana, cocaine, heroin, and methamphetamine trafficking in that era provided a basis for a rough comparison.[120] According to that report, drug-trafficking organizations' revenues from transporting marijuana through Mexico and across the U.S.-Mexico border, without netting the cost of acquiring the drug, could have amounted to $1.1 billion to $2.0 billion, and the analogous figures for cocaine, heroin, and methamphetamine could have amounted to $3.4, $1.1, and, $0.6 billion, respectively, suggesting a total of up to $7.1 billion.[121]

On that basis, our high-end, preliminary estimate of revenue from human smuggling of $2.3 billion was the same order of magnitude as RAND's earlier estimate of revenue from drug trafficking. However, as noted above, we cannot say how much of the revenue from human smuggling flows to TCOs that engage in human smuggling, as compared with other types of smugglers. Moreover, the RAND estimates for drug-trafficking revenues only included revenues from moving drugs through Mexico and across the U.S.-Mexico border and did not include revenue that drug-trafficking TCOs garner from distribution, wholesale, or retail activities that occur in the United States.

To shed additional light on the dimensions of human smuggling, we also compared revenues from human smuggling to spending on related forms of licit-market activities. Albeit another imperfect analogy, final household consumption expenditures on air, rail, truck and other transportation services in Mexico totaled almost $46 billion in 2015, making revenues from human smuggling look relatively small by comparison—about 5 percent or less—and suggesting little possibility of a noteworthy economywide effect.[122]

Improving Data Collection

Within the scope of this project, DHS asked the Homeland Security Operational Analysis Center to identify ways to improve its ability to develop estimates of revenues from human smuggling. To that end, some of the data deficiencies uncovered in this report might be insurmountable, given the illicit nature of human smuggling, but some might not be. We have identified potential improvements in data collection and methods that DHS could consider to refine the revenue estimate, reduce the breadth of the range, and better inform policymaking. Not everything can be knowable about smugglers and revenues, let alone profits, along the routes

---

[120] Kilmer et al., 2010.

[121] Kilmer et al. (2010) acknowledge that their estimates are 'substantially less than others,' but they approached revenue estimation with a well-documented and transparent methodology.

[122] Organisation for Economic Co-operation and Development (OECD) data in then-year Mexican pesos, converted using midyear exchange rates.

from the NT to the United States, but certainly more is knowable than is known already. For example:

- **DHS could standardize its line of questioning during migrant interviews across apprehension sites.** This would allow DHS to collect more consistent information about the interactions between unlawful migrants and human smugglers—including the types of smugglers they encounter and the fees they pay to smugglers.
- **DHS could seek details from migrants that would increase its ability to assess revenues, by route, and distinguish different types of smugglers and payments.** For example, DHS could ask not just "Did you use a smuggler?" and "What did you pay the smuggler?" but also "How many different smugglers did you encounter?" "Were the smugglers operating alone or with others?" "How did you come in contact with the smuggler(s)?" "Did you pay the smuggler(s) up front?" "How many payments did you make?" "What services did you receive for each of these payments?" etc. DHS might also include questions concerning the details of the route, modes of transportation, and preferences for hiring smugglers at different points along the route, such as border crossings. DHS might also seek to distinguish between fees for transit through Mexico and for transit across the U.S.-Mexico border and between those smuggling fees and drug-trafficking TCOs' taxes.
- **DHS could create a shared portal for data entry that screens for errors, if it has not done so already, and use a randomized survey process.** These actions could reduce the administrative burden of data collection on frontline personnel and increase the likelihood of successful data entry. A shared portal that provides a common interface for data entry for all U.S. Border Patrol agents and feeds into a consolidated database could be programmed to recognize inconsistencies, outliers, and other errors. Moreover, if officials interview just a random sample of unlawful migrants, they might have more time to process migrants and attend to other needs, even with additional questions.

We recognize that DHS would need to invest in developing appropriate survey instruments, training personnel to administer them consistently, and developing supporting infrastructure to implement such suggestions.

Even with the imperfect data at hand, a longer-term research project might be able to reduce some of the uncertainty of the preliminary revenue estimate, which could result in better evidence for resource allocation decisions. For example, a research team could build on the calculations in this report by taking more time to explore the sensitivity of the calculations to underlying assumptions about smugglers' and migrants' behavior, how markets operate, trends in pricing, etc. It could also explore additional ways to filter and eliminate "noise" in the data that could result from data entry problems, confusion over payments to smugglers versus other actors, and confusion over the currency that migrants use to pay smugglers.

These are just a few technical suggestions, but with greater awareness of the diversity of actors that engage in human smuggling, DHS might be able to reorient its data collection to reflect that diversity and analyze its implications for homeland security.

Appendix A. Guidance for Literature Review

We developed guidance for reviewing the literature (academic articles, press reports, and reports written by government agencies, nongovernmental organizations, and multilateral entities), consisting of instructions, search terms, parameters, and examples of relevant "hits." The guidance included a detailed outline of themes of interest and key terms pertaining to human smuggling from the NT to the United States, drawn from our discussion points for the SME interviews (discussed in Appendix B).

To start, we shared this guidance with library staff, who made a preliminary sweep through the literature in the final days of September 2018 and the first few days of October 2018. The staff used the guidance to create various threads, including, "(smuggler* OR trafficker* OR "human smuggling organization" OR "alien smuggling organization" OR "migrant smuggling organization" OR "human trafficking organization" OR "drug trafficking organization*" OR "transnational smuggling" OR coyote*) AND ("central america*" OR salvador* OR guatemala* OR hondura*) AND (cost OR costs OR piso* OR revenue* OR fee OR fees OR profit*)," and tried other combinations of terms and phrases, including "governance."

The searches covered several bibliographic databases, including Academic Search Complete, Business Search Complete, Social Science Abstracts, Criminal Justice Abstracts, Sociological Abstracts, PAIS Index, Index to Legal Periodicals, eBook Business Book Collection, EBSCO eBook Collection, ERIC, GREENFIle, MEDLINE, EconLit, US Major Dailies, Regional Business News, PsychInfo, Education Abstracts, MAS Ultra, CINAL Plus, Health Source, Military and Government Collection, and Open Source.

Upon completion of the initial sweep, we began scanning the results for relevant material, also working with the guidance.

Appendix B. Discussion Points and Questions for Subject-Matter Experts

We developed a set of discussion points and questions, formed as an outline, to guide interviews with SMEs, and slides, including a synopsis of these points and questions, as read-ahead materials for the SMEs.

The discussion points and questions are reprinted below.[123]

Human Smuggling, Transnational Criminal Organizations, and Revenues Along Routes from Northern Triangle Countries to the United States

The Nature of Transnational Criminal Organizations (TCOs) that Engage in Human Smuggling from the Northern Triangle (NT) and Across the U.S.-Mexican Border

- Where are the TCOs located?
- Do they have operatives or a presence in the United States?
- How are they structured and how big are they?
  - How centralized is decisionmaking?
  - How many employees or affiliates do they have?
  - Do they subcontract for services?
- How do they advertise their services or recruit/connect with migrants?
- To what extent—and how—do they interact with other TCOs, e.g., collaboratively, competitively, or violently?
- To what extent—and how—do they interact with law enforcement?
- Do TCOs that engage in human smuggling also engage in other criminal activities?

Extent and Form of NT Migrants' Engagement with TCOs and Other Smugglers

- What percentage of NT migrants seeks services of TCOs?
- What percentage seeks services of individual operators along the route or travel independently without such services?
- To what extent do NT migrants seek services of TCOs/others for an entire route, as compared to separate segments of a route or border crossings?
- If migrants tend to seek services for particular routes, segments, or crossing, which ones?
- How do NT migrants obtain information about TCOs and other smugglers?

[123] The discussion points and questions have been edited only slightly, largely for purposes of formatting.

Fees Charged to NT Migrants and Operating Costs

- What is the average fee a migrant from the NT pays to TCOs?
  - What is the fee for an entire route?
  - What are the fees for particular segments?
  - What is the fee just to cross into the United States?
- How do TCOs receive payment and collect fees?
  - Lump sum or installment?
  - Before departure, along the way, or upon arrival/release in the United States?
- What is included in this fee?
  - How many attempts—or trips—do they get?
  - What kind of transportation do they receive?
  - Does the fee include transportation inside the United States?
  - How do TCOs enforce payments of fees that are to be collected upon arrival/release?
- What costs do TCOs incur en route, e.g., basic transportation, food and shelter, weapons, or bribes and do migrants' fees cover them?
- How much do TCOs profit from smuggling?

TCO Tactics Along Routes from the Northern Triangle to the United States

- What routes do TCOs that engage in human smuggling typically use?
- How do those TCOs decide what route to take?
- Do they use buses, cars, trains, boats?
- How closely do they coordinate or interact with other TCOs, including those that engage in drug and/or weapon trafficking, along the routes?
- How do they choose when and where to cross the border into the United States?
- How closely do different TCOs coordinate border crossings with each other?
- Do they pay off or avoid law enforcement and, if so, how?
- Do TCOs that engage in human smuggling typically engage concurrently in other forms of smuggling, e.g., drugs or weapons, or criminal activities?
- To what extent do TCOs or other smugglers invoke violence, e.g., directed at immigrants or other smugglers, and under what circumstances?

Data Sources, Prior Studies, and Methodologies

- Are estimates of migrant flows, routes, fees, revenues, costs, etc., available in official reports (e.g., DHS), academic studies, or other documents or databases?
- Are you aware of any official reports (e.g., DHS), academic studies, or other documents that discuss any of these issues, including the fees paid by migrants and the tactics and costs borne by TCOs that engage in human smuggling?
- Are you aware of any promising methodological developments in this arena?

Appendix C. Guidance for Data Analysis

Working primarily with data from DHS,[124] and treating migrant flows from each country as "routes," we undertook aggregate revenue calculations based on the numbers of individuals traveling each route, the percentage of migrants who hire smugglers along the route, and the amount that those migrants pay smugglers to help them along the route. Simply put, revenues would equal the product of the number of migrants along each route, the percentages of those migrants who hire smugglers, and the payments, per migrant, to smugglers.

We referred to this as an "aggregate" calculation because the data do not distinguish smugglers by type, e.g., TCO, ad hoc group, or independent operator.

We developed a data analysis outline, or guidance, and embarked on estimating the flows of migrants from each of the NT countries and from the NT overall, their use of smugglers, and their payments to smugglers. In addition, we considered the extent of recidivism among unlawful migrants from each of the NT countries. The data analysis outline is reprinted below.

Data Analysis Outline[125]

Time frame is 2012–2017, by fiscal year, if corresponding to other U.S. Customs and Border Protection/DHS data regarding apprehensions, turn-backs, got-ways, smuggling costs, etc. In each case calculate for individuals traveling from each of Guatemala, Honduras, and El Salvador and the three countries combined, which is the region known as the "Northern Triangle" (NT).

1. Flows of migrants for each year, calculated as
   a. $Apprehensions_i$ (APP_i) + Observed $Got\text{-}Aways_i$ (GA_i)
   b. APP_i + Observed $Turn\text{-}Backs_i$ (TB_i) + GA_i
   c. APP_i/r_{app}
   d. $APP_i/r_{app} + TB_i$

      Where:

      i = Country (Guatemala, Honduras, or El Salvador) or region (NT).

      $GA_i = APP_i/APP_{SWB} * GA_{SWB}$

      $TB_i = APP_i/APP_{SWB} * TBS_{SWB}$

      SWB = Southwest border, between POEs

      r_{app} = estimated "partial apprehension rate" [DHS Office of Immigration Statistics, 2017, p. 8].[126]

---

[124] We also worked with EMIF Sur data on use of smugglers and smuggling fees.

[125] This outline, developed by the project team to guide the estimation process, has been edited only slightly, largely for purposes of formatting and for consistency with the use of vocabulary in the rest of the report.

Assumptions:

- Recidivism is relatively minor for the NT, pending rate results, below.
- Most NT migrants travel through SWB.
- NT country's and the NT region's share of observed turn-backs and got-aways is approximately the same as its share of recorded apprehensions.
- NT country's and the NT region's apprehension rate is about the same as the overall apprehension rate, r_{app}.[127]
- For calculations without turn-backs, someone who turns back will try again and eventually will be apprehended or get away.

2. Recidivism rates[128]
   a. Over the period 2012–2017
   b. For 2012, 2013, 2014, etc., individually
   c. For 2- or 3-year moving averages, as appropriate, pending calculations of days between contacts with border enforcement and numbers of contacts[129]
   d. For appropriate moving averages, either 2- or 3-year, create a table of 'number of tries' and 'number of individuals.'
3. Percentage of migrants that report use of smugglers.
4. Average smuggling fees, adjusted for outliers, e.g., by removing "tails."[130]
5. Median smuggling fees, without adjusting for outliers, etc.

Recidivism, Apprehension Rates, and Migrant Flows

Recidivism, which appears to be most common among Mexican nationals, can manifest in the DHS apprehension data when an unlawful migrant who is apprehended between POEs along the southwest border has been apprehended previously. (As noted above, the way to determine whether someone is a recidivist is by comparing fingerprint numbers across records in the apprehension data.) The recidivism phenomenon—namely, apprehension and re-apprehension—is closely related to the class of capture-recapture models commonly used in ecology to estimate wildlife populations, where exhaustive sampling is impractical. In the ecological context, the "recaptured" populations (like recidivists in the border security context) provide critical information for estimating the total wildlife populations (like the entire flow of illegal migrants in the border security context).

---

[126] DHS provided us with the underlying point estimates for the rate.

[127] If 2017 rate is unavailable, use 2016 rate or extrapolate from trends.

[128] Calculated as shares of unique individuals who try to enter the United States and are apprehended more than once in a given period, as specified, based on a comparison of fingerprint numbers in the apprehension data.

[129] Two-year moving averages calculated as 2012–2013, 2013–2014, 2014–2015, 2015–2016, and 2016–2017, and three-year moving averages calculated as 2012–2014, 2013–2015, 2014–2016, and 2015–2017.

[130] We set the cutoff at two standard deviations.

Espenshade first proposed the repeated trials model (RTM), in 1995, based on the capture-recapture models, to measure the flow of illegal migrants across the southwest border.[131] In addition to the flow, the RTM also estimates the apprehension rate or the probability of apprehension. In the RTM, both the flow and the apprehension rate are functions of the numbers of total apprehensions and recidivist apprehensions. To make the RTM more realistic, Chang and his co-authors later proposed a modified RTM that incorporates at-the-border deterrence, and he developed revised formulas for the flow and the apprehension rate.[132] As recidivism is mainly characteristic of Mexican nationals, Chang also suggested that the apprehension rate should be estimated by using just those records pertaining to Mexican nationals in the apprehension database. The apprehension rate thus obtained is then assumed to be applicable to the entire population.[133] Deterrence is not measured directly, and must be estimated via other means, such as surveys or econometric models. A recent Office of Immigration Statistics report, *Efforts by DHS to Estimate Southwest Border Security between Ports of Entry*, summarizes the development of the estimate of the apprehension rate and its limitations.[134]

---

[131] Espenshade, 1995, pp. 545–565.

[132] Chang et al., 2006.

[133] Whitley et al., 2016.

[134] DHS Office of Immigration Statistics, 2017.

Appendix D. DHS and EMIF Sur Data on Smuggling Fees

This appendix presents information on the properties of the data on smuggling fees from DHS and EMIF Sur in Tables D.1 and D.2.

Table D.1. Smuggling Fees Reported in DHS Data for Fiscal Year 2017

Country of Origin	Mean Fee	Median Fee	Standard Deviation	Sample Size
Guatemala	$4,725	$4,000	$4,632	6,417
Honduras	$3,777	$3,000	$2,936	4,379
El Salvador	$4,560	$4,000	$3,062	5,735

Table D.2. Smuggling Fees Reported in EMIF Sur Data for Calendar Year 2017

Country of Origin	Mean Fee	Median Fee	Standard Deviation	Sample Size
		For transit from country of origin to U.S. border		
Guatemala	$6,085	$6,164	$2,793	1,044
Honduras	$6,386	$6,500	$1,227	462
El Salvador	$3,985	$4,000	$1,525	1,081
		For transit across U.S. border		
Guatemala	$4,615	$4,110	$3,109	1,196
Honduras	$4,230	$5,000	$2,427	529
El Salvador	$4,040	$4,000	$2,305	1,486
		Totals for transit from country of origin to and across U.S. border		
Guatemala	$10,700[a]	$10,274[a]	--	--
Honduras	$10,617[a]	$11,500[a]	--	--
El Salvador	$8,025[a]	$8,000[a]	--	--

SOURCES: Author estimates based on EMIF Sur calendar-year data (EMIF, undated-a) and fiscal-year data provided by DHS.
NOTE: Cost estimates are in nominal U.S. dollars, using midyear exchange rates to adjust EMIF Sur data denominated in non-U.S. currencies (e.g., pesos or quetzals). Figures might not add due to rounding.
[a] These figures are the sums of the means or medians, respectively, for each country for each segment, first, from the country of origin to the U.S. border and, second, across the U.S. border.

References

Amnesty International, *Mexico: Invisible Victims. Migrants on the Move in Mexico*, 2010. As of November 29, 2018: https://www.amnesty.org/en/documents/AMR41/014/2010/en/

Associated Press, "Human Smugglers Cash In on Central American Migration to U.S.," CBC News website, July 21, 2014. As of October 28, 2018: https://www.cbc.ca/news/world/human-smugglers-cash-in-on-central-american-migration-to-u-s-1.2712878

Beittel, June S., *Mexico: Organized Crime and Drug Trafficking Organizations*, Washington, D.C.: Congressional Research Service, R41576, July 3, 2018.

Burnett, John, "Migrants Say They're Unwilling Mules for Cartels," NPR website, December 4, 2011. As of October 28, 2018: https://www.npr.org/2011/12/04/143025654/migrants-say-theyre-unwilling-mules-for-cartels

Cabrera, Chris, testimony on behalf of the National Border Patrol Council before the U.S. Senate Homeland Security and Governmental Affairs Committee, Washington, D.C., October 21, 2015. As of November 8, 2018: https://www.hsgac.senate.gov/imo/media/doc/Testimony-Cabrera-2015-10-21.pdf

Caldwell, Alicia A., "U.S. Border Crossings Are Fewer, Riskier and More Expensive," *Wall Street Journal*, October 5, 2018

Campana, Paolo, "The Structure of Human Trafficking: Lifting the Bonnet on a Nigerian Transnational Network," *British Journal of Criminology*, Vol. 56, No. 1, 2016, pp. 68–86.

Castellano, Laura, "Devoran Coyotes Millones con Niños," *El Universal*, July 29, 2014. As of October 29, 2018: http://www.pressreader.com/mexico/el-universal/20140729/281530814157297

Chang, Joseph C., R. Kohout, H. R. Blacksten, and S. Bernard, *CBP Apprehensions at the Border*, Arlington, Va.: Homeland Security Institute, HSI Publication Number RP05-25f-04, 2006.

Cleek, Ashley, "With Smuggling Costs Skyrocketing, Parents Balance Risk and Debt for Their Children's Future," Public Radio International website, February 28, 2018. As of November 7, 2018: https://www.pri.org/stories/2018-02-28/smuggling-costs-skyrocketing-parents-balance-risk-and-debt-their-childrens-future

Daily Mail and Associated Press Reporters, "From Bribing Drug Cartels and Immigration Officials to Paying for Hotels and Train Rides: Coyote Smugglers Reveal Costs Involved in Smuggling Child Migrants from Central America to the U.S.," *Daily Mail*, July 22, 2014. As of October 18, 2018: https://www.dailymail.co.uk/news/article-2700946/From-bribing-drug-cartels-immigration-officials-paying-hotels-train-rides-Coyote-smugglers-reveal-costs-involved-smuggling-child-migrants-Central-America-U-S.html

Domingo Villegas, Rodrigo, "Central American Migrants and 'La Bestia': The Route, Dangers, and Government Responses," *Migration Policy Institute*, September 10, 2014. As of November 18, 2018: https://www.migrationpolicy.org/article/central-american-migrants-and-"la-bestia"-route-dangers-and-government-responses

Egan, Dennis, Paul Kantor, Fred Roberts, Vladimir Menkov, and Katie McKeon, "Estimating Missed Detections at the Southern Border," unpublished presentation at George Mason University by the Borders, Trade, and Immigration Institute: A DHS Center of Excellence led by the University of Houston, via subcontract to Rutgers, 2018.

EMIF, homepage, undated-a. As of November 28, 2018: https://www.colef.mx/emif/eng/index.php#

EMIF, "Surveys of Migration at Mexico's Northern and Southern Borders: Background and Objective," El Colegio de la Frontera Norte website, undated-b. As of November 8, 2018: https://www.colef.mx/emif/eng/antecedentes_objetivos.php

EMIF, "Surveys of Migration at Mexico's Northern and Southern Borders: Research Methodology," El Colegio de la Frontera Norte website, undated-c. As of November 8, 2018: https://www.colef.mx/emif/eng/bases_metodologicas.php

EMIF Sur, "Indicadores Anuales 2017," COLEF.mx website, p. 5, Chart 9b, 2018a. As of November 8, 2018: https://www.colef.mx/emif/resultados/indicadores/indicadores/Sur/2017/Anual/SUR-Indicadores-ANUALES%202017.pdf

EMIF Sur, "Indicadores Semestrales EMIF Sur: OCT 2017-MZO 2018," COLEF.mx website, March 2018b. As of November 8, 2018: https://www.colef.mx/emif/resultados/indicadores/indicadores/Sur/2017/S1/SUR-Indicadores-S1-oct2017-marzo2018.pdf

Espenshade, Thomas J., "Using INS Border Apprehension Data to Measure the Flow of Undocumented Migrants Crossing the U.S.-Mexico Frontier," *International Migration Review*, Vol. 29, No. 2, 1995, pp. 545–565.

Farah, Douglas, and Pamela P. Lum, *Central American Gangs and Transnational Criminal Organizations: The Changing Relationships in a Time of Turmoil*, Washington, D.C.: International Assessment and Strategy Center, February 2013.

Finckenauer, James O., *Chinese Transnational Organized Crime: The Fuk Ching*, Washington, D.C.: National Institute of Justice, 2001. As of November 7, 2018: https://www.ncjrs.gov/pdffiles1/nij/218463.pdf

Frontline/World, "Extended Interview: A Human Smuggler," PBS website, 2018. As of October 13, 2018: http://www.pbs.org/frontlineworld/stories/mexico704/interview/smuggler.html

Gallagher, Mike, "Drugs, Guns and People: Smuggling Is a Growing Border Problem," *Albuquerque Journal*, June 10, 2018. As of October 28, 2018: https://www.abqjournal.com/1183179/drugs-guns-and-people-smuggling-is-a-growing-border-problem.html

Garsd, Jasmine, "Human Smuggler: Central Americans Are Worth Their Weight in Gold," transcript, NPR website, January 28, 2016. As of November 7, 2018: https://www.npr.org/2016/01/28/464664750/human-smuggler-central-americans-are-worth-their-weight-in-gold

González, Daniel, and Gustavo Solis, "The Wall: A Human Smuggler, and the Wall That Will Make Him Rich," *USA Today*, 2017. As of October 28, 2018: https://www.usatoday.com/border-wall/story/human-smuggling-crossing-border-illegally-methods/559784001/

Guevara González, Yaatsil, "Navigating with Coyotes: Pathways of Central American Migrants in Mexico's Southern Borders," *Annals of the American Academy of Political and Social Science*, Vol. 676, No. 1, March 2018, pp. 174–193.

Hale, Gary J., Adam N. Hale, Nathan P. Jones, and Russell Lundberg, "Uncovering Human Trafficking Patterns from Guatemala to the U.S.," unpublished presentation at George Mason University by the Borders, Trade, and Immigration Institute: A DHS Center of Excellence led by the University of Houston, 2018.

Hennessy-Fiske, M., "Migrants, Young and Old, Are Not Always Related; Border Patrol Says Fear of Child Trafficking Forces Separations," *Los Angeles Times*, May 8, 2018. As of November 7, 2018: http://www.latimes.com/nation/la-na-border-patrol-dna-20180508-htmlstory.html

International Crisis Group, *Easy Prey: Criminal Violence and Central American Migration*, Report 57, July 2016.

Kilmer, Beau, Jonathan P. Caulkins, Brittany M. Bond, and Peter H. Reuter, *Reducing Drug Trafficking Revenues and Violence in Mexico: Would Legalizing Marijuana in California Help?* Santa Monica, Calif.: RAND Corporation, OP-325-RC, 2010. As of November 14, 2018: https://www.rand.org/pubs/occasional_papers/OP325.html

Kulish, Nicholas, "What It Costs to Be Smuggled Across the U.S. Border," *New York Times*, June 30, 2018. As of October 24, 2018: https://www.nytimes.com/interactive/2018/06/30/world/smuggling-illegal-immigration-costs.html

Leutert, Stephanie, "When Drug Trafficking Is Your Only Option," *Foreign Policy*, July 14, 2017.

Leutert, Stephanie, *Organized Crime and Central American Migration in Mexico*, Lyndon B. Johnson School of Public Affairs, Policy Research Project 198, 2018.

Martinez, Oscar, "Los Coyotes del Norte Están Aumentando las Cuotas por TRUMP," *Animal Politico*, February 10, 2017. As of October 28, 2018: https://www.animalpolitico.com/2017/02/coyotes-migracion-trump/

McAuliffe, Marie, and F. Laczko, *Migrant Smuggling Data and Research: A Global Review of the Emerging Evidence Base*, Geneva, Switzerland: International Organization for Migration, 2016.

Miroff, Nick, "The Border Is Tougher to Cross Than Ever. But There's Still One Way into America," *Washington Post*, October 24, 2018. As of November 21, 2018: https://www.washingtonpost.com/graphics/2018/national/border-asylum-claims/?utm_term=.c35364dae56d

Morral, Andrew R., Henry H. Willis, and Peter Brownell, *Measuring Illegal Border Crossing Between Ports of Entry: An Assessment of Four Promising Methods*, Santa Monica, Calif.: RAND Corporation, OP-328-OSD, 2011. As of November 14, 2018: https://www.rand.org/pubs/occasional_papers/OP328.html

Nixon, R., and T. Heisler, "High Profits and Misery Meet at Door of Smugglers' Stash Houses," *New York Times*, August 26, 2018. As of November 7, 2018: https://www.nytimes.com/2018/08/26/us/politics/smugglers-border-immigrants-money.html

Olson, Eric L., *Migrant Smuggling and Trafficking at the Rio Grande Valley: Ten Observations and Questions*, Washington, D.C.: The Wilson Center, September 2016. As of November 8, 2018: https://www.wilsoncenter.org/sites/default/files/olson_border_2016_0.pdf

Organisation for Economic Co-operation and Development, *Can We Put an End to Human Smuggling?* Paris, France, MPD No. 9, December 2015.

Palacios, S. P. Izcara, "Coyotaje and Drugs: Two Different Businesses," *Bulletin of Latin American Research*, Vol. 34, No. 3, December 30, 2014, pp. 324–329.

Paoli, Letizia, and V. Greenfield, "The Supply of Doping Products and the Relevance of Market-Based Perspectives: Implications of Recent Research in Italy," in Jens Beckert and Matias Dewey, eds., *Everything Legal? Interfaces Between legality and Illegality in Markets*, Oxford: Oxford University Press, 2017, pp. 245–267.

Paoli, Letizia, V. Greenfield, and P. Reuter, *The World Heroin Market: Can Supply Be Cut?* New York: Oxford University Press, 2009.

Paoli, Letizia, V. Greenfield, and A. Zoutendijk, "The Harms of Cocaine Trafficking: Applying a New Framework for Assessment," *Journal of Drug Issues*, Vol. 43, No. 4, 2013, pp. 407–436.

Pelley, Scott, correspondent, CBS News, transcript of *60 Minutes* episode, "Human Smuggling Across the Southern Border; Desperation and Fear Are Driving a Dangerous Industry That's Virtually Impossible to Completely Stop," March 11, 2018. As of October 28, 2018: https://www.cbsnews.com/news/human-smuggling-across-the-southern-border/

Prendergast, Curt, "Costly Crossing Fees Turn Illegal Immigrants into Marijuana Smugglers," *Arizona Daily Star*, April 8, 2017. As of October 29, 2018: https://tucson.com/news/local/border/costly-crossing-fees-turn-illegal-immigrants-into-marijuana-smugglers/article_1e95e570-080c-5dd7-a240-687cce94ca8f.html

Reuter, Peter, and V. Greenfield, "Measuring Global Drug Markets: How Good Are the Numbers and Why Should We Care About Them?" *World Economics*, Vol. 2, No. 4, October–December 2001, pp. 159–173.

Roberts, Bryan, G. Hanson, D. Cornwall, and S. Borger, *An Analysis of Migrant Smuggling Costs Along the Southwest Border*, Washington, D.C.: U.S. Department of Homeland Security, Office of Immigration Statistics, working paper, November 2010.

Rodríguez Chávez, Ernesto, *Migración centroamericana en tránsito irregular por México. Nuevas cifras y tendencias*, Instituto Tecnológico Autónomo de México (ITAM)/El Colegio de la Frontera Norte (Colef), PB #14, December 2016.

Sanchez, Gabriella, "Latin America," in Marie McAuliffe and Frank Laczko, eds., *Migrant Smuggling Data and Research: A Global Review of the Emerging Evidence Base*, Geneva, Switzerland: International Organization for Migration, 2016, pp. 269–301.

Sanchez, Gabriella, "Critical Perspectives on Clandestine Migration Facilitation: An Overview of Migrant Smuggling Research," *Journal on Migration and Human Security*, Vol. 5, No. 1, 2017, pp. 9–27.

Sanchez, Gabriella, "Five Misconceptions About Migrant Smuggling," *Migration Policy Center*, Issue 2018/07, May 2018.

Sanchez, Gabriella E., and Sheldon. X. Zhang, "Rumors, Encounters, Collaborations, and Survival: The Migrant Smuggling–Drug Trafficking Nexus in the U.S. Southwest," *Annals of the American Academy of Political and Social Science*, Vol. 676, No. 1, 2018.

Slack, Jeremy, and Howard Campbell, "On Narco-Coyotaje: Illicit Regimes and Their Impacts on the US-Mexico Border; Sociology and Anthropology," *Antipode*, Vol. 48, No. 5, 2016.

Slack, Jeremy, and Scott Whiteford, "Caught in the Middle: Undocumented Migrant's Experiences with Drug Violence," in T. Payan, K. Staudt, and Z. A. Kruszewski, eds., *A War That Can't Be Won: Binational Perspectives on the War on Drugs*, Tucson, Ariz.: University of Arizona Press, 2013, pp. 193–213.

Tiempo.hn, "Human Smugglers Charge at Least $7,000 to Take Migrants to US," in Spanish, August 7, 2017. As of November 7, 2018: https://tiempo.hn/compatriotas-necesitan-7-mil-dolares-coyote-eeuu/

United Nations Office on Drugs and Crime, *Legislative Guide for the Implementation of the United Nations Convention Against Transnational Organized Crime*, Vienna, Austria, 2004. As of October 25, 2018: http://www.unodc.org/documents/treaties/Legislative_Guide_2017/Legislative_Guide_E.pdf

United Nations Office on Drugs and Crime, *Smuggling of Migrants: A Global Review and Annotated Bibliography of Recent Publications*, New York, 2011.

United States, Executive Office of the President, *Strategy to Combat Transnational Organized Crime: Addressing Converging Threats to National Security*, Washington, D.C.: Executive Office of the President, July 2011.

U.S. Code, Title 10: Armed Forces; Subtitle A: General Military Law; Part I: Organization and General Military Powers; Chapter 15: Military Support for Law Enforcement Agencies; Section 284: Support for counterdrug activities and activities to counter transnational organized crime.

U.S. Department of Homeland Security, Office of Immigration Statistics, *Efforts by DHS to Estimate Southwest Border Security Between Ports of Entry*, Washington, D.C., 2017. As of October 23, 2018: https://www.dhs.gov/sites/default/files/publications/17_0914_estimates-of-border-security.pdf

U.S. Department of Justice, Drug Enforcement Administration, *2017 National Drug Threat Assessment*, DEA-DCT-DIR-040-17, Washington, D.C., October, 2017.

U.S. Immigration and Customs Enforcement, "41 Arrested in Multinational Human Smuggling Takedown in Central America and South America," Washington, D.C., July 8, 2016. As of November 7, 2018: https://www.ice.gov/es/news/releases/41-arrested-multinational-human-smuggling-takedown-central-america-and-south-america

Weden, Axel Storen, "Deadly Human Trafficking Business on Mexico-US Border," *Al Jazeera*, January 24, 2016. As of November 7, 2018: https://www.aljazeera.com/indepth/features/2016/01/deadly-human-trafficking-business-mexico-border-160117073423022.html

Whitley, John E., J. W. Bailey, S. K. Burns, D. F. Eisler, C. C. Fletcher, T. P. Frazier, B. R. Gould, K. M. Guerrera, T. C. Heuring, B. Q. Rieksts, and B. Roberts, *Assessing Southern Border Security*, Arlington, Va.: Institute for Defense Analyses, IDA Paper NS P-5304, 2016.

Wuebbels, Mark, "Demystifying Human Smuggling Operations Along the Arizona-Mexican Border," 2004. As of October 13, 2018: http://traccc.gmu.edu/pdfs/publications/human_trafficking_publications/wuebbe01.pdf

Zhang, Sheldon X., *Smuggling and Trafficking in Human Beings: All Roads Lead to America*, Westport, Conn.: Praeger, 2007.

Zhang, Sheldon X., "The United States," in Marie McAuliffe and Frank Laczko, eds., *Migrant Smuggling Data and Research: A Global Review of the Emerging Evidence Base,* Geneva, Switzerland: International Organization for Migration, 2016, pp. 303–324.